Footprint Handbook

Ke

DAVID

This is
Kerala

Route planner

Kerala's shape keeps planning simple: there's a limited choice of main routes, and it's easy to build a general-purpose itinerary that allows plenty of chances to indulge in special interests, whether they be natural, cultural, culinary or simply chilling out on a beach.

Highlights

beaches, backwaters, tea plantations and Ayurvedic healing

Two weeks is plenty of time to travel Kerala end to end, taking in a good sample of the state's scenic and cultural highlights. Fly into Thiruvananthapuram and get your India legs with a couple of relaxed days at the beach in Kovalam or Varkala. After a night or two afloat on a backwaters houseboat, head inland and climb the winding hill road to Periyar National Park. Explore the park on foot or by the early morning cruise, then travel north to Munnar, where cool air and tea plantations await. From here, dive down to the coast again and spend some time exploring the lanes of Fort Kochi. It's a short train ride from here to the River Nila, where you could check in for a few days of Ayurvedic healing and explore the cultural attractions of the area, then finish off by heading north to Kannur for beaches and Theyyam dances.

Wildlife

bamboo rafting and a jungle treehouse

Starting from Kochi or Thiruvananthapuram, head for Periyar National Park, which offers the best wild elephant spotting in the state. Allow two full days, including a day for the excellent hiking and bamboo rafting trip on Lake Periyar. From here aim for Munnar to visit Eravikulam National Park, home to the endangered Nilgiri tahr, and perhaps dip across the Tamil Nadu border to search for leopards in Chinnar Wildlife Sanctuary. Return to the coast via Thattekad Bird Sanctuary, and travel north to the Silent Valley National Park, whose untouched forests are home to the rare great hornbill and lion-tailed macaque. Finish off with a couple of nights in a jungle treehouse in Wayanad.

When to go

Climate

By far the most comfortable time to visit Kerala is from October to March, when the weather is dry and relatively cool. April and May are intensely hot, especially on the coastal plains, with humidity building up as the monsoon approaches. The southwest monsoon hits Kerala in early June, sweeping northward up the coast; the heaviest rain comes in July and can see large parts of the state knee-deep in water for hours or even days at a time. A second, lighter monsoon begins in September or October, travelling up the east coast. If you're travelling during the monsoon you need to be prepared for extended periods of torrential rain and disruption to travel. The post-monsoon period brings cool air and clear skies – this is the best time for mountain views – while winter temperatures can drop close to zero in the higher terrain of the Western Ghats.

Weather Thiruvananthapuram

January	February	March	April	May	June
31°C	31°C	32°C	32°C	31°C	29°C
22°C	23°C	24°C	25°C	25°C	24°C
23mm	22mm	36mm	110mm	210mm	343mm

July	August	September	October	November	December
29°C	29°C	30°C	30°C	30°C	30°C
23°C	24°C	24°C	24°C	23°C	23°C
219mm	143mm	152mm	268mm	199mm	70mm

India has a wealth of festivals with many celebrated nationwide, while others are specific to a particular state or community or even a particular temple. Many fall on different dates each year depending on the Hindu lunar calendar; there's a thorough calendar of upcoming major and minor festivals at www.drikpanchang.com. Local festivals are listed in the Festivals section throughout the book.

The Hindu calendar

Hindus follow two distinct eras: The *Vikrama Samvat* which began in 57 BC and the *Salivahan Saka* which dates from AD 78 and has been the official Indian calendar since 1957. The *Saka* new year starts on 22 March and has the same length as the Gregorian calendar. The 29½ day lunar month with its 'dark' and 'bright' halves based on the new and full moons, are named after 12 constellations, and total a 354-day year. The calendar cleverly has an extra month (*adhik maas*) every 2½ to three years, to bring it in line with the solar year of 365 days coinciding with the Gregorian calendar of the West.

Some major national and regional festivals are listed below. A few count as national holidays: **26 January**: Republic Day; **15 August**: Independence Day; **2 October**: Mahatma Gandhi's Birthday; **25 December**: Christmas Day.

Major festivals and fairs

1 January New Year's Day is accepted officially when following the Gregorian calendar but there are regional variations which fall on different dates, often coinciding with spring/harvest time in March and April.

13-16 January The four-day harvest festival of **Pongal** is celebrated with great fervour in areas with a large Tamil population. Doorsteps are decorated with *kaolam* (geometric designs in coloured powder), cattle are worshipped, and vast pots of the eponymous rice dish are cooked

February Vasant Panchami, the spring festival when people wear bright yellow clothes to mark the advent of the season with singing, dancing and feasting.

February-March Maha Sivaratri marks the night when Siva danced his celestial dance of destruction (*Tandava*), which is celebrated with feasting and fairs at Siva temples, but preceded by a night of devotional readings and hymn singing.

April Vishu is Kerala's New Year, when houses are decorated with lights and firecrackers explode in the air. Pilgrims flock to the temples of Sabarimala and Guruvayur. Kerala's **Pooram** season reaches full swing, with elephant parades, fireworks and cacophonous drumming in honour of the goddess

Kali. The climax of the season is the huge **Thrissur Pooram**.

April/May Buddha Jayanti, the 1st full moon night in April/May marks the birth of the Buddha.

July/August Snake boat races take place all over the backwaters.

15 August is **Independence Day**, a national secular holiday is marked by special events. **Vinayaka Chaturthi,** known elsewhere in India as **Ganesh Chaturthi**, is the day when the elephant-headed god of good omen is shown special reverence. On the last of the five-day festival after harvest, clay images of Ganesh are taken in procession with dancers and musicians, and are immersed in the sea, river or pond.

August/September Kerala's 'national festival', **Onam**, takes place over 10 days, with great processions (the biggest takes place in Thripunithara, a suburb of Kochi), snake boat races and sumptuous feasts.

August/September Janmashtami, the birth of Krishna is celebrated at midnight at Krishna temples.

September/October The festival of **Navaratri** has many local variations throughout India. Kerala's version is based around worship of Saraswathi, the goddess of wisdom and learning. Books are worshipped, and on the tenth day (*Dasara*), children are officially initiated into reading and writing. Parades take place in Thiruvanathapuram.

October/November Gandhi Jayanti (**2 October**), Mahatma Gandhi's birthday, is remembered with prayer meetings and devotional singing.

Diwali/Deepavali (*Sanskrit ideepa* lamp), the festival of lights, is celebrated particularly in North India. Some Hindus celebrate Krishna's victory over the demon Narakasura, some Rama's return after his 14 years' exile in the forest when citizens lit his way with oil lamps. The festival falls on the dark *chaturdasi* (14th) night (the one preceding the new moon), when rows of lamps or candles are lit in remembrance, and *rangolis* are painted on the floor as a sign of welcome. Fireworks have become an integral part of the celebration which are often set off days before Diwali. Equally, Lakshmi, the Goddess of Wealth (as well as Ganesh) is worshipped by merchants and the business community who open the new financial year's account on the day. Most people wear new clothes; some play games of chance.

25 December Christmas Day sees Indian Christians celebrate the birth of Christ in much the same way as in the West; many churches hold services/Mass at midnight. There is an air of festivity in city markets which are specially decorated and illuminated.

31 December Over **New Year's Eve** hotel prices peak and large supplements are added for meals and entertainment in the upper category hotels. Some churches mark the night with a Midnight Mass, while the beach resorts of Varkala and Kovalam throw wild parties. Fort Kochi celebrates with a full-blown **Portugese Carnival**, culminating at midnight with the lighting of a giant effigy of Santa.

Muslim holy days

These are fixed according to the lunar calendar. According to the Gregorian calendar, they tend to fall 11 days earlier each year, dependent on the sighting of the new moon.

Ramadan is the start of the month of fasting when all Muslims (except young children, the very elderly, the sick, pregnant women and travellers) must abstain from food and drink, from sunrise to sunset. Ramadan is most widely observed in the Malabar region of northern Kerala; during this time many restaurants remain closed until sundown.

Id ul Fitr is the three-day festival that marks the end of Ramadan.

Id-ul-Zuha/Bakr-Id is when Muslims commemorate Ibrahim's sacrifice of his son according to God's commandment; the main time of pilgrimage to Mecca (the Hajj). It is marked by the sacrifice of a goat, feasting and alms giving.

Muharram is when the killing of the Prophet's grandson, Hussain, is commemorated by Shi'a Muslims. Decorated *tazias* (replicas of the martyr's tomb) are carried in procession by devout wailing followers who beat their chests to express their grief. Hyderabad and Lucknow are famous for their grand *tazias*. Shi'as fast for the 10 days.

What to do

from relaxation and yoga to whitewater rafting

Ayurveda and yoga

Kerala has set itself up as one of India's leading health destinations, with some of the country's most luxurious and most authentic Ayurvedic spas – though those two qualities don't generally go hand in hand. In every town with any sort of traveller activity you'll find various places offering casual yoga classes and Ayurvedic treatments, ranging from bliss-outs such as *shirodhara* (a steady stream of warm oil poured onto your forehead) to vigorous *kalari* massage, carried out by a masseur hanging from ropes and mashing your muscles with the full strength of his legs. The gold standard is *panchkarma*, a complete oil change and service for your body that in its purest form takes three weeks, with treatments tailored to your precise needs by qualified doctors; a wonderful experience, but one that you'll need to commit to fully to get the most benefit from. Kovalam has a string of high-end Ayurvedic resorts, as do Varkala and Fort Kochi to a lesser extent, though some say that pore-blocking salt air reduces the power of the treatments. The River Nila region is another hotspot, with a selection of superb and authentic retreats, some set in ancient manor houses. Wherever you go, most massage places use the traditional hard wooden beds – which can be hell on your backbone after an hour's pummelling.

Birdwatching

The state's diverse and rich natural habitats harbour almost 500 species of bird. On the plains, the cooler months (November-March) are the most comfortable for a chance to see migratory birds from the hills, but the highlands are ideal between April and June and again after the monsoons when visibility improves in October and November. Water bodies large and small draw visiting waterfowl from other continents during the winter.

Some prime birding spots include Ponmudi, Periyar National Park, Munnar, the RAMSAR-listed marshes around Thrissur, Lake Vembanad, Thattekad Bird Sanctuary and Wayanad. *Birds of the Indian Subcontinent*, by Grimett, Inskipp and Inskipp, is an excellent general-puropose field guide.

For information, try local websites such as www.birdsofkerala.com, or www.orientalbirdclub.org, and www.cloudbirders.com for recent trip reports.

Houseboats

These icons of Kerala ply the network of waterways around Lake Vembanad, sections of which can at times feel utterly jammed with houseboats. The main departure points for houseboat cruises are Alappuzha, Kumarakom and Kollam, with the typical houseboat trip involving a tour around the canals near Alleppey, a tootle across Lake Vembanad, an overnight stay on board and visits to various local 'attractions' – mostly shops dressed up as coconut plantations. It can be worth going on a two-night cruise, which gets you further away from the crowds and provides more time to settle into the steady rhythm of backwaters life. For a less mainstream alternative, try a cruise on the quieter Valiaparamba backwaters in north Kerala.

Watersports

Parasailing, windsurfing and waterskiing are popular in Kovalam, and the beach town also offers a somewhat anaemic surfing scene. For underwater sports, the only really worthwhile destination is the Lakshadweep Islands, two hours by air from Kochi, which offer Maldives-style coral atolls with virtually no other tourists. However, at present the Lakshadweeps offer no dive facilities – you would need to be totally self sufficient – and only a tiny choice of very basic government-run tent 'resorts'. Securing a permit to visit is also a tricky and time-consuming job.

Whitewater rafting

Kerala's whitewater circuit is limited to the Tejaswini River, which flows down from Coorg to meet the Arabian Sea near Kannur. This is leisurely rafting, mostly at Grade II with a few Grade III stretches in the lower reaches. A more rustic alternative is to try bamboo rafting, in which a few logs of bamboo are lashed to inner tubes and set loose on a lake or gently bubbling river. Top spots for this include the River Nila and Periyar National Park.

Shopping tips

India excels in producing fine crafts at affordable prices through the tradition of passing down ancestral skills. A good place to shop for handicrafts is from government-owned emporia such as **Kairali** in Kochi and **SMSM Emporium** in Thiruvanananthapuram. These shops offer guaranteed quality at fixed prices (no bargaining), but many are dimly lit with items poorly displayed, a fact not helped by sometimes reluctant and unenthusiastic staff. Private upmarket shops and top hotel arcades offer better quality, choice and service but at a price. Vibrant and colourful local bazars are often a great experience but you must be prepared to bargain.

Bargaining can be fun and quite satisfying but it is important to get an idea of prices being asked by different stalls for items you are interested in, before taking the plunge. Some shopkeepers will happily quote twice the actual price to a foreigner showing interest, so you might well start by halving the asking price. On the other hand it would be inappropriate to do the same in an established shop with price tags, though a plea for the 'best price' or a 'special discount' might reap results even here. Remain good humoured throughout. Walking away slowly might be the test to ascertain whether your custom is sought and you are called back.

Warnings Some taxi/rickshaw drivers and tour guides will endeavour to take you to certain shops, where the owners pay them a commission on every item you buy. Small private shops can't always be trusted to pack and post your purchases: unless you have a specific recommendation from a person you know, only make such arrangements in government emporia or a large store. Make sure, too, that credit cards are run off just once when making a purchase. Don't enter into any arrangement to help 'export' marble items, jewellery or gem stones, no matter how well-spoken your would-be trading partner nor how lucrative your cut of the profits may sound; these are invariably scams that suddenly involve you spending thousands on your credit card.

Export of antiquities and art objects over 100 years old is restricted. Ivory, musk, skins of all animals, *shahtoosh* wool and articles made from them are banned, unless you get permission for export. For further information, contact the Indian High Commission or consulate, or check www.cbec.gov.in.

Carpets and dhurries

The superb hand-knotted carpets of Kashmir, using old Persian designs woven in wool or silk or both, are hard to beat for their beauty and quality. You'll find Kashmiri traders wherever there's a hint of foreign tourism, most notably in Fort Kochi and Kovalam.

Jewellery

Advertising hoardings for jewellery stores loom over every bend in Kerala's roads, and opulent gold wedding jewellery is one of the State's biggest businesses. It's best to buy from reputable shops as street stalls often pass off fake ivory, silver, gems and stones as real. Gold and silver should have a hallmark, but antique pieces often do not.

Metal work

Bell metal, an alloy of tin, copper and brass, is used to cast temple bells and oil lamps as well as mythological portrayals of the Gaja Tandava, Shiva's dance of cosmic destruction.

Paintings

You can buy portable versions of Kerala's traditional religious mural paintings from artists in Kochi, Thiruvanathapuram and Guruvayur.

Textiles

Rich shot silk from Kanchipuram is one of South India's best buys. If you look hard enough you'll also find skilful *ikat* from Gujarat, brocades from Varanasi, colourful Rajasthani block-printed cottons and sober handspun *khadi*, not to mention the ubiquitous *pashmina* shawl and scarf from Kashmir.

Wood craft

Each region of India has its special wood, and Kerala's are sandalwood and rosewood. You'll find them carved into fine wooden panels and images, as well as mass-produced elephants and snake boats.

Where to stay

India has an enormous range of accommodation, and you can stay safely and very cheaply by Western standards right across the country. The mainstay of the budget traveller is the ubiquitous Indian 'business hotel'. These are usually within walking distance of train and bus stations, anonymous but generally decent value, with en suite rooms of hugely variable cleanliness and a TV showing 110 channels of cricket and *Bollywood MTV*. At the top end, alongside international chains like **ITC Sheraton** (ostentatious) and **Radisson Blu** (dependable), India boasts several home-grown hotel chains, best of which are the exceptional heritage and palace hotels operated by the **Taj** group.

Meanwhile, Kerala offers abundant opportunities to stay in fine style in converted mansions and farmhouses – a great way to help preserve architectural heritage while keeping your money in the local economy. While the coastal holiday belts of southern Kerala have their share of big and bland resorts, you'll also find a huge variety of individual lodgings, from porous coconut-fibre beach shacks that don't even come with a lock, to luxurious restored forts overlooking the Arabian Sea and minimalist Zen retreats hidden in paddy fields.

In the high season (October to April, peaking at Christmas/New Year and again at Easter) bookings can be extremely heavy in popular destinations such as Kovalam and Varkala. It is generally possible to book in advance by phone, fax or email, sometimes on payment of a deposit, but double check

Price codes

Where to stay	
$$$$	over US$150
$$$	US$66-150
$$	US$30-65
$	under US$30

For a double room in high season, excluding taxes.

Restaurants	
$$$	over US$12
$$	US$6-12
$	under US$6

For a two-course meal for one person, excluding drinks or service charge.

your reservation a day or two beforehand and always try to arrive as early as possible in the day to iron out problems.

Price categories

The category codes used in this book are based on prices of double rooms excluding taxes. They are not star ratings and individual facilities vary considerably. Modest hotels may not have their own restaurant but will often offer 'room service', bringing in food from outside; in temple towns, restaurants may only serve vegetarian food.

Off-season rates

Large reductions are made by hotels in all categories out-of-season in many resorts. Always ask if any is available. You may also request the 10-15% agent's commission to be deducted from your bill if you book direct. Clarify whether the agreed figure includes all taxes.

Taxes

In general most hotel rooms rated at Rs 1200 or above are subject to a tax of 10%. Many states levy an additional luxury tax of 10-25%, and some hotels add a service charge of 10% on top of this. Taxes are not necessarily payable on meals, so it is worth settling your meals bill separately. Most hotels in the $$ category and above accept payment by credit card. Check your final bill carefully. Visitors have complained of incorrect bills, even in the most expensive hotels. The problem particularly afflicts groups, when last-minute extras appear mysteriously on some guests' bills. Check the evening before departure, and keep all receipts.

Hotel facilities

You have to be prepared for difficulties which are uncommon in the West. It is best to inspect the room and check that all equipment (air conditioning, TV, water heater, flush) works before checking in at a modest hotel. Many hotels try to wring too many years' service out of their linen, and it's quite common to find sheets that are stained, frayed or riddled with holes. Don't expect any but the most expensive or tourist-savvy hotels to fit a top sheet to the bed.

In some states **power cuts** are common, or hot water may be restricted to certain times of day. The largest hotels have their own generators but it is best to carry a good torch.

In some regions **water supply** is rationed periodically. Keep a bucket filled to use for flushing the toilet during water cuts. Occasionally, tap water may be discoloured due to rusty tanks. During the cold weather and in hill stations, hot water will be available at certain times of the day, sometimes in buckets, but is usually very restricted in quantity. Electric water heaters may provide enough for a shower but not enough to fill a bath tub. For details on drinking water, see page 23.

Hotels close to temples can be very noisy, especially during festivals. Music blares from loudspeakers late at night and from very early in the morning, often making sleep impossible. Mosques call the faithful to prayers at dawn. Some find ear plugs helpful.

Some hotels offer **24-hour checkout**, meaning you can keep the room a full 24 hours from the time you arrive – a great option if you arrive in the afternoon and want to spend the morning sightseeing.

Homestays

At the upmarket end, increasing numbers of travellers are keen to stay in private homes and guesthouses, opting not to book large hotel chains that keep you at arm's length from a culture. Instead, travellers get home-cooked meals in heritage houses and learn about a country through conversation with often fascinating hosts. Kerala has been particularly enthusiastic in embracing the homestay model, although the term is increasingly abused as a marketing term by small hotels. Companies specializing in homestays include Kerala Connections ⓘ www.keralaconnections.co.uk, MAHout ⓘ www.mahoutuk.com, Pyramid Tours ⓘ www.pyramidtravelindia.com, and Sundale Vacations ⓘ www.sundale.com.

Food
& drink

from masala dosa to spicy fish stew with coconut milk

Food

You'll find just as much variety in dishes crossing South India as you would on an equivalent journey across Europe. Varying combinations of spices and unique local ingredients give each region its distinctive flavour.

Kerala's cultural and religious diversity means that vegetarian food is less dominant than in the neighbouring states of Tamil Nadu and Karnataka. The two pillars of Kerala cuisine are coconut and the indigenous *matta* rice, a distinctively nutty and nutritious variety often served with its husk.

Typical dishes you'll find throughout Kerala include *appam* (a moist, crisp-edged pancake of rice flour fermented with palm toddy or wine), *idiyappam* (steamed rice flour noodles), and *puttu* (hard cylindrical cakes of rice flour and grated coconut). All of the above are generally served at breakfast with a coconut-cream based stew of meat, fish or vegetables, and washed down with Kerala's brew of choice, milky filter coffee.

Along the Kerala coast, with its largely Syrian Christian and Muslim population, you'll find excellent fish and seafood dishes. Commonly found fish include *pearlspot* and *karimeen*, and these might be served simply fried, grilled or steamed, or in a *meen molee* (a potently spiced stew laden with coconut milk and tapioca).

Also ubiquitous throughout the state are the humble snacks that appear on menus in South Indian cafés the length and breadth of India: *masala dosa* (a crispy rice pancake folded over and stuffed with a lightly spiced potato filling), *utthapam* (a cross between a pancake and a pizza, topped with tomato and onion or slices of banana), and *idli* (soft steamed rice cakes served with a spicy stew called *sambar* and coconut chutney). Every town has a slew of places serving these staples, and for less than US$1 you can fuel yourself up for a full morning's sightseeing.

Throughout India the best-value food comes in the shape of the traditional *thali* (called 'meals' in Kerala and neighbouring Tamil Nadu), a complete feast often served on a banana leaf. Several curries surround the central serving of rice. A typical lunchtime *thali* will include *sambar* (thick lentil and vegetable soup), *rasam* (a hot peppery consommé) two or three curries which can be quite hot and maybe a crisp poppadum. A variety of pickles are offered – mango and lime are two of the most popular. These can be exceptionally hot, and are designed to be taken in minute quantities alongside the main dishes. Plain *dahi* (yoghurt), or *raita*, usually acts as a bland 'cooler', and there's usually a bowl of sweet *payasam* (rice pudding) to finish off.

If you're unused to spicy food, go slow. Food is often spicier when you eat with families or at local places, and certain cuisines (notably those of Andhra Pradesh and the Chettinad region of Tamil Nadu) are notorious for going heavy on the chilli. Most restaurants are used to toning things down for foreign palates, so if you're worried about being overpowered, feel free to ask for the food to be made less spicy.

Food hygiene has improved immensely in recent years. However, you still need to take extra care, as flies abound and refrigeration in the hot weather may be inadequate and intermittent because of power cuts. It is safest to eat only freshly prepared food by ordering from the menu (especially meat and fish dishes). Be suspicious of salads and cut fruit, which may have been lying around for hours or washed in unpurified tap water – though salads served in top-end hotel restaurants and places primarily catering to foreigners (eg in Fort Kochi, Varkala and Kovalam) can offer a blissful break from heavily spiced curries.

Choosing a good restaurant can be tricky if you're new to India. Many **local eateries** sport a grimy look that can be off-putting, yet serve brilliant and safe food, while swish five-star hotel restaurants that attract large numbers of tourists can dish up buffet food that leaves you crawling to the bathroom in the middle of the night. A large crowd of locals is always a good sign that the food is freshly cooked and good. Even fly-blown *dhabas* on the roadside can be safe, as long as you stick to freshly cooked meals and avoid timebombs like deep-fried samosas left in the sun for hours.

Many city restaurants and backpacker eateries offer a choice of so-called **European options** such as toasted sandwiches, stuffed pancakes, apple pies, fruit crumbles and cheesecakes. Italian favourites (pizzas, pastas) can be very different from what you are used to. Ice creams, on the other hand, can be exceptionally good; there are excellent Indian ones as well as some international brands.

India has many delicious tropical **fruits**. Some are seasonal (eg mangoes, pineapples and jackfruit), while others (eg bananas, grapes and oranges) are available throughout the year. It is safe to eat the ones you can wash and peel.

Don't leave India without trying its superb range of indigenous **sweets**. A piece or two of milk-based *peda* or Mysore *pak* make a perfect sweet postscript to a cheap dinner.

Drink

Drinking water used to be regarded as one of India's biggest hazards. It is still true that water from the tap or a well should never be considered safe to drink since public water supplies are often polluted. Bottled water is now widely available although not all bottled water is mineral water; most are simply purified water from an urban supply. Buy from a shop or stall, check the seal carefully and avoid street hawkers; when disposing bottles puncture the neck which prevents misuse but allows recycling.

There is growing concern over the mountains of plastic bottles that are collecting and the waste of resources needed to produce them, so travellers are being encouraged to carry their own bottles and take a portable water filter. It is important to use pure water for cleaning teeth.

Tea and coffee are safe and widely available. Both are normally served sweet, and with milk. If you wish, say 'no sugar' (*chini nahin*), 'no milk' (*dudh nahin*) when ordering. Alternatively, ask for a pot of tea and milk and sugar to be brought separately. Freshly brewed coffee is a common drink in South India, but in the North, ordinary city restaurants will usually serve the instant variety. Even in aspiring smart cafés, espresso or cappuccino may not turn out quite as you'd expect in the West.

Bottled soft drinks such as Coke, Pepsi, Teem, Limca and Thums Up are universally available but always check the seal when you buy from a street stall. There are also several brands of fruit juice sold in cartons, including mango, pineapple and apple – Indian brands are very sweet. Don't add ice cubes as the water source may be contaminated. Take care with fresh fruit juices or *lassis* as ice is often added.

Tender coconut water is available at roadside stalls everywhere, and makes for a deliciously cooling natural refresher. Another good option for rehydration is a sweet/salted lime soda.

Indians rarely drink alcohol with a meal. In the past wines and spirits were generally either imported and extremely expensive, or local and of poor quality. Now, the best Indian whisky, rum and brandy (IMFL or 'Indian Made Foreign Liquor') are widely accepted, as are good Champenoise and other wines from Maharashtra. If you hanker after a bottle of imported wine, you will only find it in the top restaurants or specialist liquor stores for at least Rs 1000.

As of 2014, Kerala has begun phasing in alcohol prohibition. Around half of the State's bars were denied licenses in 2014, and another 300 were closed down in 2015. At the time of writing, alcohol is only officially available through five-star hotel bars and government-owned liquor shops, though the latter are also being closed down at a rate of 10% per year; the laws don't affect shops selling locally produced palm *toddy*.

As usual in India, the reality is more fluid, and travellers report being served beer and spirits in tea pots in humble hotels and bars.

FOOD AND DRINK

Menu reader

Styles of cooking

bhoona in a thick, fairly spicy sauce

chops minced meat, fish or vegetables, covered with mashed potato, crumbed and fried

cutlet minced meat, fish, vegetables formed into flat rounds or ovals, crumbed and fried (eg prawn cutlet, flattened king prawn)

do piaza with onions (added twice during cooking)

dum pukht steam baked

jhal frazi spicy, hot sauce with tomatoes and chillies

Kashmiri cooked with mild spices, ground almonds, yoghurt and fruit

kebab skewered (or minced and shaped) meat or fish; a dry spicy dish cooked on a fire

kima minced meat (usually 'mutton')

kofta minced meat or vegetable balls

korma in fairly mild rich sauce using cream/yoghurt

masala marinated in spices (fairly hot)

Madras hot

makhani in butter rich sauce

molee/moilee South Indian dishes cooked in coconut milk and green chilli sauce

Mughlai rich North Indian style

Nargisi dish using boiled eggs

navratan curry ('nine jewels') colourful mixed vegetables and fruit in mild sauce

Peshwari rich with dried fruit and nuts (northwest Indian)

tandoori baked in a tandoor (special clay oven) or one imitating it

thoran dry curry with shredded coconut

tikka marinated meat pieces, baked quite dry

Ularthiyathu dry-fried with spices

Typical North Indian dishes

aloo gosht potato and mutton stew

aloo gobi dry potato and cauliflower with cumin

aloo, matar, kumbhi potato, peas, mushrooms in a dryish mildly spicy sauce

bhindi bhaji okra fried with onions and mild spices

biriyani partially cooked rice layered over meat and baked with saffron

boti kebab marinated pieces of meat, skewered and cooked over a fire

dhal makhani lentils cooked with butter

dum aloo potato curry with a spicy yoghurt, tomato and onion sauce

khichari rice and lentils cooked with turmeric and other spices

matar panir curd cheese cubes with peas and spices (and often tomatoes)

murgh massallam chicken in creamy marinade of yoghurt, spices and herbs with nuts

nargisi kofta boiled eggs covered in minced lamb, cooked in a thick sauce

pulao/pilau fried rice cooked with spices (cloves, cardamom, cinnamon) with dried fruit, nuts or vegetables.

rogan josh rich, mutton/beef pieces in creamy, red sauce

sag panir drained curd (panir) sautéed with chopped spinach in mild spices

sarson-ke-sag and **makkai-ki-roti** mustard leaf cooked dry with spices served with maize flour roti from Punjab

shabdeg a special Mughlai mutton dish with vegetables

yakhni lamb stew

Typical South Indian/Keralan dishes

appam spongy white pancake made of fermented rice flour, often served with coconut milk or mildly spiced stew

avial vegetable curry based on coconut

beef ularthiyathu Syrian Christian dish, dry cooked with spices

fish molee coconut based fish curry

idiyappam/string hoppers steamed rice flour noodles

meen mulakittathu fish in hot red chilli sauce

pachadi yoghurt-based vegetable curry

puttu steamed cylinders of ground rice layered with coconut

rasam peppery consommé

sambar thin and spicy vegetable gravy served with dosa, idly and vadai

stew mild creamy coconut milk curry

upma thick and spicy semolina "porridge", much more delicious than it sounds

Roti – breads

chapati (roti) thin, plain, wholemeal unleavened bread cooked on a *tawa* (griddle), usually made from *ata* (wheat flour). **Makkaiki roti** is with maize flour.

nan oven baked (traditionally in a tandoor) white flour leavened bread often large and triangular; sometimes stuffed with almonds and dried fruit

paratha fried bread layered with *ghi* (sometimes cooked with egg or potatoes)

poori thin deep-fried, puffed rounds of flour

porotta – flaky flat bread used to mop up curries.

Sweets

These are often made with reduced/thickened milk, drained curd cheese or powdered lentils and nuts. They are sometimes covered with a flimsy sheet of decorative, edible silver leaf.

barfi fudge-like rectangles/diamonds

gulab jamun dark fried spongy balls, soaked in syrup

halwa rich sweet made from cereal, fruit, vegetable, nuts and sugar

khir, payasam, paesh thickened milk rice/vermicelli pudding

kulfi cone-shaped Indian ice cream with pistachios/almonds, uneven in texture

jalebi spirals of fried batter soaked in syrup

laddoo lentil-based batter 'grains' shaped into rounds

rasgulla (roshgulla) balls of curd in clear syrup

sandesh dry sweet made of curd cheese

Snacks

bhaji, pakora vegetable fritters (onions, potatoes, cauliflower, etc) deep-fried in batter

chat sweet and sour fruit and vegetables flavoured with tamarind paste and chillies

chana choor, chioora ('Bombay mix') lentil and flattened rice snacks mixed with nuts and dried fruit

dosai South Indian pancake made with rice and lentil flour; served with a mild potato and onion filling (masala dosai) or without (ravai or plain dosai)

idly steamed South Indian rice cakes, a bland breakfast given flavour by spiced accompaniments

kachori fried pastry rounds stuffed with spiced lentil/peas/potato filling

samosa cooked vegetable or meat wrapped in pastry triangles and deep fried

utthappam thick South Indian rice and lentil flour pancake cooked with spices/onions/tomatoes

vadai deep fried, small savoury lentil 'doughnut' rings. **Dahi vada** are similar rounds in yoghurt

Essential Kerala

Finding your feet

Stretching from some of the highest mountains of the Western Ghats to the lush coastal plain, Kerala (area 39,000 sq km, population 33.3 million) encapsulates the rich diversity of western India's coastal landscapes. Its narrow coastal fringe has been raised from the sea in the last million years. Inland are rolling hills of laterite, succeeded by the ancient rocks that form the backbone of the Western Ghats.

Getting around

Kerala is famous for its converted rice boat backwaters tours; take the ferry for a more local route around. Bus and car journeys in the backwaters are picturesque too. There are trains from Malabar to Ernakulam and on to Trivantharapuram.

When to go

It's hot all year round. Kerala does not have an extended totally dry season characteristic of the rest of India, but is particularly wet during the monsoon season, from June to September, when many places close. March and April are stiflingly hot. High season is November-March; outside this time prices may drop by up to 50%. Trekking is best December-April. Check www.keralatourism.org/festivalcalendar.php for exact festival dates.

Time required

Two days is enough for a backwaters cruise. Leave a couple of days for Fort Kochi and a few in Varkala. A week will make Malabar a worthwhile detour. Add three days for a wildlife trip into the Ghats, in Periyar or Wayanad.

Food and drink

Kerala's cuisine reflects its diverse religious traditions, its location on the seaboard and the ubiquitous presence of the coconut. Uniquely in India, beef is widely eaten, although seafood is far more common. Fish *moilee* is prepared with coconut milk and spices while for *pollichathu* the fish is baked with chilli paste, curry leaves and spices. Coconut-based dishes such as *thoran*, a dry dish of mixed vegetables chopped very small, herbs and curry leaves, and *avial*, similar to *thoran* but cooked in a sauce, are widely eaten. *Erisseri* is a thick curry of banana or yam and *kichadi* is beetroot or cucumber in coconut-curd paste. You can try these with the soft centred, lacy pancake *appam* or the soft noodle rice cakes *iddiappam*.

Jack fruit, pineapples, custard apples and an endless variety of bananas also play a vital part in many dishes. For dessert, you might get milk *payasam*, made with rice or vermicelli.

Thiruvananthapuram
& the far south

The state capital, a pleasant city built over gently rolling coastal land, is very much a village as soon as you step away from the crowded centre. There's none of the throb, bustle and boom-time of Ernakulam, its opposite city up north, and no one could accuse it of being cosmopolitan; you'll be pushed to find a club, or bar, or even any traffic on the roads after midnight.

It is, however, a stone's throw from here to the white sands of Kovalam, still a working fishing village, albeit one that survives under the lengthening shadow cast by unchecked tourist development. The backpackers who first populated Kovalam have left it to the package holidaymakers and luxury resorts and head instead to Varkala, a pilgrimage village and beach marked out by its sheer red rock face. Inland are the little-visited forests of Ponmudi and just over the southern border lies Kanniyakumari, the sacred toe-tip of India where three seas converge.

Essential Thiruvananthapuram and the far south

Finding your feet

The international airport is 6 km from the centre of Thiruvananthapuram, a 15-minute drive outside rush hour, and half an hour from Kovalam. You can hire a prepaid taxi (Rs 200-300) or auto (about Rs 100) into town or wait for a local bus. At the southern end of Thiruvananthapuram are the central (long-distance) bus station, with services throughout Kerala and into neighbouring Tamil Nadu, and the railway station from where trains run up and down the coast.

Best budget hotels

Manjalikulam Tourist Home, Thiruvananthapuram, page 36
Coco Land, Kovalam, page 44
Hotel Greenland, Kovalam, page 44
Marine Palace, Varkala, page 50
Sea Pearl Chalets, Varkala, page 50

Local buses in Thiruvananthapuram, including those bound for Kovalam, leave from the East Fort City stand opposite the fort entrance, southwest of the station. Buses to Kovalam can drop you at Waller Junction, five minutes' walk from the Samudra Beach hotels. A further 1.5 km on they turn off for the main Kovalam Bus Stand at the Ashok Hotel gate, five minutes from most southern hotels and cafés. Lighthouse Road is steep and narrow, but autos and taxis are able to drive up it. For details, see Transport, page 39.

Fact...
The name Thiruvananthapuram is derived from Tiru Ananta Puram, the abode of the sacred serpent Ananta upon whose coils Vishnu lies in the main temple.

Best Ayurvedic resorts

Niraamaya, near Kovalam, page 43
Somatheeram Ayurvedic Beach Resort, Chowara Beach, page 44
Dr Franklin's Panchakarma Institute and Research Centre, Chowara, page 46

Getting around

With a population of 1,687,300, Thiruvananthapuram is relatively strung out, though the centre is compact. Autos or taxis are more convenient than the packed buses but bargain hard: businesses have fast acclimatized to the price naivety that goes hand in hand with package tourism. Minimum charges start at Rs 150 for taxis, Rs 20 for autos; thereafter the rate per running kilometre for cars is Rs 12 (non-a/c), Rs 15 (a/c), rickshaws Rs 10. Drivers may be reluctant to accept the going rate. If you're heading for Kovalam, budget on around Rs 250 for a taxi and Rs 175 for an auto.

Tip...
When shopping, bear in mind that prices are relatively high in this region. Traders seldom honour the standard rates for 92.5ct silver, charging by piece not weight.

Useful contacts
Foreigners' Regional Registration Office, City Police Commissioner, Residency Road, Thycaud, T0471-232 0579; allow up to a week for visas, though it can take less. Monday-Saturday 1000-1700.

Sights

Sri Padmanabhaswamy Temple ⓘ *East Fort, T0471-245 0233, open 0330-0445, 0630-0700, 0830-1000, 1030-1110, 1145-1200, 1700-1815 and 1845-1920.* According to legend, the Sri Padmanabhaswamy Temple was built in stages to house the statue of Vishnu reclining on the sacred serpent Ananta, which was found in the forest. It was rebuilt in 1733 by Raja Marthanda Varma, king of the erstwhile kingdom of Travancore, who dedicated the whole kingdom, including his rights and possessions, to the deity. The full significance of this gift came to light in July 2011, after Kerala's High Court ordered the Travancore royal family to hand over control of the temple and its assets to the State. Upon opening the six *kallaras* (vaults) hidden beneath the temple, a team of archaeologists discovered a hoard of gold- and jewel-encrusted idols estimated to be worth at least US$22 billion in weight alone. The find instantly propelled the temple to the head of the list of India's richest religious institutions. Meanwhile, in a twist fit for Indiana Jones, a sixth vault, guarded by an iron door emblazoned with images of cobras, remains sealed while the Supreme Court and temple astrologers wrestle over legends of a powerful curse set to be unleashed if the door is ever prised open.

Unusually for Kerala, the temple is built in the Dravidian style associated with Tamil Nadu, with beautiful murals, sculptures and 368 carved granite pillars which support the main pavilion or *kulashekharamandapa*. You can see the seven-storeyed *gopuram* with its sacred pool from outside; otherwise to get a closer look you first have to persuade the famously strict Kerala Brahmins to waive the Hindus-only entry restriction. It becomes easier to do so if men have donned a crisp white *dhoti*, women a sari and blouse.

Kuthiramalkia (Puthenmalika) Palace ⓘ *Just next to the temple, Temple Rd, East Fort, T0471-247 3952, Tue-Sun 0830-1330 and 1500-1730, Rs 20, camera Rs 15.* The Travancore king, Maharajah Swathi Thirunal Balarama Varma, was a musician, poet and social reformer, and his palace is a fine reflection of his patronage of the arts. On the upper level a window gives an angle on scores of fine wood-carved horses that look like a huge cavalry charge, and among the portraits painted in the slightly unsettling Indian/European classical hybrid style is one from an artist who trumped his rivals by painting not just eyes that follow you around the room, but also feet. Sadly, it is ill maintained, but a gem nonetheless.

Napier Museum ⓘ *North Park Grounds, city north, T0471-231 8294, Tue-Sun 1000-1645, Wed morning only, closed public holidays.* The museum building is a spectacular landmark. Designed by RF Chisholm in traditional-Kerala-meets-Indo-Saracenic style, it was completed in 1872. Today, it houses a famous collection of eighth to 18th-century South Indian bronzes, mostly from Chola, Vijayanagar and Nayaka periods, a few Jain and Buddhist sculptures and excellent woodcarvings.

Thiruvananthapuram (Trivandrum)

To Kollam (NH 17)

To Ponmadi

Sri Chitra Art Gallery

Zoo

PMG Circle **3**

LMS Junction

Napier Museum & Open Air Theatre

Museum Rd

University Stadium

Crafts Design Centre

Swimming Pool

New State Assembly

Christ

Public Library

VELLAYAMBALAM

Police Stadium

St Joseph's Cathedral

KUNNUKUZHI

Palayam Junction

Town Hall

Tagore Theatre

University College

Connemara

VAZHUTAKKAD

General Hospital Circle

Spencer Junction **1**

Central Survey Office

Accountant General's Office

Bakery Junction

Yoga Centre

Statue Rd

Statue Junction **7**

Secretariat

Kairali Handicrafts **2**

Central Stadium

Panavila Junction

Jaihind Travels

Foreigners' Registration Office

Aries Travel

SMSM Handicrafts

VANCHIYOOR

Pulimudu Junction **5** **8**

Press Rd

Housing Board Junction

THYCAUD

4

Mahatma Gandhi Rd

Ayurvedic College

Aristo Rd

Residency (KITTS)

Ayurvedic College Junction

Lab Supplies **6** **3**

THAMPANOOR

KSRTC Thampanoor Bus Stand

2

Mettukkada Mukku

Taikkad Junction

S S Coil Rd

Aristo Junction **9**

To Airport

Chettikulangara Rd

Central Station Rd

Mahalikulam Rd

1

1

Thampanoor Junction

Hospital Rd

VALIYASHALA

To 6 & Airport

Overbridge

Thakaraparambu Rd

Power House Junction

Power House Rd

SRI VENKATESWARAM

Verma Travels

Padmavilasam Rd

Fort Bus Station

EAST FORT

Sri Padmanabhaswamy Temple

FORT

Kuthiramalika Palace

To Airport

Buses to Kovalam

To Kovalam Beach (16 km)

N

200 metres
200 yards

Where to stay
Asha **11**
Capital **4**
Chaithram **1**
Greenland **2**
Highland **3**
Manjikulam Tourist Home **6**
Residency Tower **8**
Thamburu International **9**
Thapovan Heritage Home **12**
Wild Palms Homestay **10**
Youth Hostel **7**

Restaurants
Arul Jyoti **2**
Indian Coffee House **1**
Kalavara **5**
Kerala House **7**
Mascot **3**
Queen's **4**
Villa Maya **6**

Sri Chitra Art Gallery ① *Just north of the museum, 1000-1645, closed Mon and Wed mornings, Rs 5.* The Sri Chitra gallery has a fine catalogue of Indian art from early to modern schools: works by Raja Ravi Varma, 20th-century pioneer of the radical post-colonial school of painting, sit among paintings from Java, Bali, China and Japan, Mughal and Rajput miniatures. The Tanjore paintings are studded with semi-precious stones.

Zoological park ① *Entrance at southwest corner of park, Tue-Sun 0900-1815, Rs 10, cameras Rs 25.* Set in a hilly woodland of frangipani and jacaranda, the zoological park has a wide collection of animals and a well-labelled botanical garden.

East of Thiruvananthapuram

At the foot of the Western Ghats, 30 km east of Thiruvananthapuram, the **Neyyar Wildlife Sanctuary** ① *free, speedboat for 2 people Rs 250/400, larger boats to view the forests enclosing the lake Rs 25 per person,* occupies a beautiful wooded and hilly landscape, dominated by the peak of Agasthya Malai (1868 m). The vegetation ranges from grassland to tropical, wet evergreen. Wildlife includes gaur, sloth bear, Nilgiritahr, jungle cat, sambar deer, elephants and Nilgiri langur; the most commonly seen animals are lion-tailed macaques and other monkeys. Tigers and leopards have also been reported. **Neyyar Dam** supports a large population of crocodiles and otters; a crocodile farm was set up in 1977 near the administrative complex.

Immediately to the northeast of the Neyyar Wildlife Sanctuary a section of dense forest, **Agasthya Vanam**, was set aside as a biological park in 1992 to recreate biodiversity on a wide scale. Nearby, the **Sivananda Yoga Vedanta Dhanwantari Ashram** ① *T0471-227 3093, www.sivananda.org/neyyardam, minimum stay 3 days,* runs highly regarded meditation and yoga courses. It is quite an intensive schedule, with classes that start just after dawn and a strict timetable including karma yoga (meditation or devotion to God through physical labour). It is only really suitable for the hardy; others may find it heavy on Hinduism and Indian diet.

Further north sits **Ponmudi** ① *buses from Trivandrum, Thampanoor Bus Stand 0530-1630; return 0615-1905, 2½ hrs,* the nearest hill station to Thiruvananthapuram, 65 km away. In a spectacular and peaceful setting, the tourist complex, though basic, serves as a good base for trekking, birdwatching and visiting the nearby minimalist deer park.

Tourist information

Kerala Tourism
Park View, T0471-232 1132, www.
keralatourism.org. Mon-Sat 1000-1700.
Thiruvananthapuram's main tourist
office, where you can book half-day
tours around the city (Rs 300). There
are also offices at Thampanoor Central
Bus Station, the railway station and the
airport. Tourist offices have plenty of
leaflets and information sheets and are
very helpful.

Where to stay

$$$ Thapovan Heritage Home
18 km south of town, Nellikunnu,
T0471-248 0453, www.thapovan.com.
Rooms in beautiful gardens or
overlooking Nellikunu Beach. Ayurvedic
treatments, yoga, restaurant.

$$ The Capital, off MG Rd
Near the GPO, Pulimood, T0471-301 2301,
www.thecapital.in.
Renovated business hotel, with smallish
but clean rooms and some large,
excellent value suites. Excellent
rooftop restaurant. Friendly.

$$ Residency Tower
Press Rd, T0471-233 1661,
www.residencytower.com.
Top-quality a/c rooms in a business
hotel, with full facilities. Highly efficient,
good restaurants, bar, rooftop pool
(non-residents Rs 350). A bit swish.

$$ Wild Palms On Sea
Beach Rd, T0471-275 6781,
www.wildpalmsonsea.com.
Modern welcoming guesthouse wih
pool right by the beach. Spacious rooms,
some a/c. Price includes breakfast.

$$-$ Chaithram (KTDC)
Station Rd, T0471-233 0977,
www.ktdc.com.
Very clean decent-sized rooms, all a/c.
Next to railway and bus stand so can be
noisy. Restaurant, bar.

$$-$ Highland
Manjalikulam Rd, T0471-233 2645,
www.highland-hotels.com.
Rs 1100-2300 (plus taxes). Busy hotel
with a wide variety of clean rooms.
Budget rooms are good value.

$$-$ Thamburu International
Aristo Junction, T0471-232 1974,
www.thamburu.com.
Quiet, well-run hotel with wood-panelled
walls and cheesy music in the foyer.
Rooms (all with TV) tend to be on the
small side. Some a/c rooms have balcony.

$ Greenland
Aristo Junction, T0471-232 3485.
Great-value rooms in quiet, immaculate,
freshly renovated hotel, perfectly
located within a couple of mins of
both bus and railway stations. Best
budget choice in town.

$ Manjalikulam Tourist Home
Manjalikulam Rd, T0471-233 0776,
www.manjalikulam.com.
Quiet yet central hotel with large,
spotlessly clean 36 rooms. Very friendly
staff. Good value, recommended.

$ Youth Hostel (YHAI)
10 km from the centre, Veli, T0471-250 1230, youthhostelveli@gmail.com.
Rooms and a dorm surrounded by coconut groves, with a pretty lagoon and clean beach. Very cheap vegetarian lunches, boating, watersports, good views.

East of Thriuvananthapuram

$$$$-$$$ Duke's Forest Lodge
Anappara, near Ponmudi, T0472-285 9273, www.dukesforestlodge.in. Rs 5500-8500 (plus taxes).
5 luxury villas, each with its own plunge pool, set on organic estate. Also 4 standard rooms. Great trekking.

$$-$ Government Guest House
Ponmudi, T0471-289 0211. Rs 600 (plus taxes).
24 rooms and 10 cottages ($$), in attractive gardens surrounded by wooded hills, spartan facilities but spacious rooms, restaurant serves limited but reasonable vegetarian meals, beer available, also a post office and general store.

Restaurants

$$$ Villa Maya
Airport Rd, Subash Nagar, Injakkal Westfort Rd, T0471-257 8901, www.villamaya.in.
One of the most beautiful restaurants in Kerala, set in a restored 18th-century Dutch villa surrounded by fountains. Dishes span a broad range of cuisines, from traditional Kerala curries to Israeli or Moroccan specials. It's pricey and they don't serve alcohol, but this is a superb choice for a splurge.

$$ Kalavara
Kalavara Hotel, Press Rd, T0471-272 7034.
Indian, Continental, Chinese, fast food (burgers, shakes), takeaway. Food average, slow service but good-value buffets in upstairs thatched section with a patch of garden. Good ambience, limited views.

$$ Kerala House
Near Statue Junction, T0471-247 6144.
Kerala cuisine in the basement of shopping complex. Slow for breakfast but newspapers available, outside seating in the evening in roadside car park area is cheaper. Colourful and fun place to pass some time, even if the food arrives cold. Try *neem, kappa* and rice (delicious fish with tapioca), or inexpensive chicken dishes with coconut; bakery in the complex does excellent samosas and puffs.

$$ Mascot
Mascot Hotel, Museum Rd, www.mascothotelthiruvananthapuram.com.
Excellent lunchtime buffet, pleasant, 24-hr coffee shop for all types of snacks, good value, a cool haven at midday.

$ Arul Jyoti
MG Rd, opposite Secretariat.
South Indian vegetarian. With a/c family room, clean, wide choice of good-value dishes, try jumbo *dosas*. Great Tamil Nadu *thalis*.

$ Indian Coffee House
2 branches on MG Rd, T0471-321 4501, www.indiancoffeehouse.com, with others near YWCA, north of the Secretariat, and near KSRTC Bus Stand (the latter designed by the English architect Laurie Baker).
Worth seeing, excellent value coffee and snacks.

Entertainment

Performances of *Kalarippayattu*, Kerala's martial art, can be seen through: **CVN Kalari** (East Fort, T0471-247 4182, 0430-0830); and **Balachandran Nair Kalari Martial Arts Gymnasium** (Parasuvaikal, T0471-223 2686, www.kalari.in).

Festivals

Mar Chandanakuda, at Beemapalli, a shrine on Beach Rd, 5 km southwest of the railway station. 10-day festival when local Muslims go to the mosque, holding incense sticks and pots. Marked by sword play, singing, dancing, elephant procession and fireworks.

Mar-Apr (Meenam) and Oct-Nov (Thulam) **Arattu** is the closing festival of the 10-day celebrations of the Padmanabhaswamy Temple, in which the deity is paraded around the temple inside the fort and then down to the sea.

Sep/Oct Navaratri at the special *mandapa* in Padmanabhaswamy Temple. Several concerts are held which draw famous musicians. **Thiruvonam week** in Sep.

1-10 Oct Soorya Dance Festival.

Nov-Mar A similar **Nishangandhi Dance Festival** is held at weekends when all-important classical Indian dance forms are performed by leading artistes at Nishagandhi open-air auditorium, Kanakakkunnu Palace.

Shopping

Shopping areas include the **Chalai Bazar**, the **Connemara Market** and the main road from Palayam to the East Fort. Usually open 0900-2000 (some take a long lunch break). Although ivory goods have now been banned, inlay on woodcarving and marquetry using other materials (bone, plastic) continue to flourish. *Kathakali* masks and traditional fabrics can be bought at a number of shops.

The shopping centre opposite East Fort Bus Stand has a large a/c shop with a good selection of silks and saris but is not cheap. *Khadi* is recommended from shops on both sides of MG Rd, south of Pulimudu Junction.

Co-optex, *Temple Rd*. Good for fabrics and *lungis*.
Handloom House, *diagonally across from Partha's*. Has an excellent range of fabrics, clothes and export quality dhurries.
Partha's, *towards East Fort*. Recommended.
Raymonds, *KaralKada, East Fort*. Good selection of men's clothing plus pricy tailoring.

Handicrafts

Gift Corner and **Natesan Antique Arts**, *MG Rd*. High-quality goods including old dowry boxes, carved wooden panels from old temple 'cars', miniature paintings and bronzes.
Gram Sree, *MG Rd*. Excellent village crafts.
Kairali, *MG Rd*. Items of banana fibre, coconut, screw pine, mainly utilitarian, also excellent sandal-wood carvings and bell-metal lamps, utensils.
Kalanjali, *Palace Garden, across from the museum*. Recommended.
SMSM Handicrafts Emporium, *behind the Secretariat*. Government-run, heaps of items reasonably priced.

What to do

Body and soul
Institute of Yogic Culture, *Vazhuthacaud, T0471-304 9349, www.pillaisyogicculture.com.* Yoga therapy, Ayurvedic massage.
Sivananda Ashram, *Neyyar Dam, T(0)9495-630951, www.sivananda.org.in/ neyyardam.* One of India's most highly regarded yoga teacher training programs.
Vasudeva Vilasam, *Vasudeva Vilasam Rd, East Fort, T0471-409 1000, www. vasudeva.com.* Simple but with experienced professionals.

Swimming
Mascot Hotel, *Cantonment Rd, www. mascothotelthiruvananthapuram.com.* Has a big pool.
Waterworks, *near the museum, T0471-231 8990.* Has a pool.

Tour operators
The following are IATA-approved agencies.
Great India Tour Co, *New Corporation Building, Palayam, T0471-301 1500, www. gitc.travel.* Offers afternoon city tours, among others. Reliable but pricey.
KTDC, *Hotel Chaithram, Station Rd, T0471-233 0031, www.ktdc.com.* Can arrange 2- to 3-day tours to Munnar and Thekkady and also runs the following local tours: **City tour**: daily 0800 and 1330, 5½ hrs including Padmanabhapuram, Puthenmalika Palace, Shangumugham beach and Napier Museum, Rs 300 (Padmanabhapuram is closed on Mon).
Kanniyakumari: daily 0730-2100, including Kovalam, Padmanabhapuram and Kanniyakumari, Rs 700. Tours can feel quite rushed with little time spent at sights.

TourIndia, *MG Rd, T0471-233 0437, www.tourindiakerala.com.* The pioneers of backwater tourism and Periyar's Tiger Trails trekking program. Highly recommended for innovative and unusual experiences, eg treehouse holidays or sport fishing off Fort Kochi.

Trekking and birdwatching
Trekking is best Dec-Apr. Obtain permission first from the Chief Conservator of Forests (Wildlife), Forest HQ, Thiruvananthapuram, T0471-232 5385, or the Assistant Wildlife Warden at Neyyar Dam, T0471-227 2182.

Transport

Air The airport, T0471-250 1591, is 6 km west of the centre. There are banks and money exchange facilities including **Thomas Cook**, T0471-250 2470. Transport to town is by local bus no 14, prepaid taxi (Rs 150) or auto (about Rs 100, 20 mins). Prepaid taxis to **Kovalam** cost around Rs 350. Banks at the airport are outside Arrivals. Note that the terminal is closed at night.

Domestic flights to most major Indian cities including: **Bengaluru**, **Chennai**, **Delhi**, **Hyderabad**, **Kochi**, **Kolkata**, **Kozhikode** and **Mumbai**.

International departures include: **Air India Express** to several **Gulf** destinations; **Emirates** to **Dubai**; **Etihad** to **Abu Dhabi**. **Maldivian** to **Malé**; **Silk Air** and **Tiger Airways** to **Singapore**; **Sri Lankan** to **Colombo**.

Bus Local: City Bus Stand, T0471-257 5495. Green buses have limited stops; yellow/red buses continue through town up to museum. Blue/white bus (No 888) to **Kovalam** goes from **East Fort Bus Station** (30 mins, Rs 9).

Long distance: Buses leave from **KSRTC Bus Station**, Station Rd, near railway station, T0471-232 3886, www.keralartc.com. Buses to **Kanniyakumari** via **Nagercoil** or direct, 0530, 0930, 1000, 1200, 1500, 1600 and 1830 (2½ hrs) and frequent departures to **Kozhikode** (10 hrs) via **Kollam** (2½ hrs), **Alappuzha** (4 hrs), **Ernakulam/Kochi** (5½ hrs) and **Thrissur** (7 hrs). You can take in a section of the backwaters on the way to Kochi by getting a boat from Kollam. **SETC** buses leave for destinations in Tamil Nadu, including **Chennai** (12 hrs), **Coimbatore** (8 hrs), **Kanniyakumari** and **Madurai** (7 hrs).

Rickshaw Rickshaws to the **Kovalam** beach area should cost around Rs 150-170. You will need to bargain. Tell auto-rickshaw drivers which beaches you want to get to in advance, otherwise they will charge much more when you get there.

Taxi From town, taxis charge about Rs 12 per km; to **Kovalam**, Rs 290, return Rs 580 (waiting: extra Rs 50 per hr). To **Kanniyakumari** with a stop at **Padmanabhapuram** costs about Rs 1500/2000.

Train Central Station, T132. Reservations in the building adjoining the station; for foreign tourist quota bookings, go to Counter 8 upstairs, open 0700-1300, 1330-1930, Sun 0900-1700; ask to see the Chief Reservations Supervisor. To **Bengaluru**: 2 daily, 18 hrs; **Chennai**: 4 daily, 15 hrs; **Ernakulam** (Kochi): around 20 trains daily, 5¼ hrs, all via **Varkala** (40 mins) and **Kollam** (1 hr); most continue via **Kottayam**, 3 hrs; some via **Alleppey**, 2½ hrs. To **Kanniyakumari**: 4 daily, 2½ hrs. To **Mangalore**: 6 daily, 13 hrs, via **Ernakulam**, **Thrissur** (5½ hrs), **Kozhikode** (7½ hrs) and **Kannur** (10 hrs).

Local fishermen's boats still sit on Kovalam's narrow strip of sand right next to sunbathing tourists, but the sleepy Lakshadweep seaside village of old has now been almost completely swallowed up by package tourist infrastructure: Ayurveda parlours, trinkets, tailoring shops and tour operators line every inch of the narrow walkways behind the shore. In peak season it's something of an exotic god's waiting room, popular with pensioners, and it's safe and sedate enough for families. Backpackers tend to return off season.

Beaches

North and south of Kovalam (population 25,400) are four main stretches of beach, about 400 m long, divided by a rocky promontory on which sits the Charles Correa-designed **Leela Hotel**. The area to the north of the promontory, known as **Samudra Beach** and **Pozhikara Beach**, 5 km away offers the most sheltered bathing and the clearest water. The southern beaches, **Lighthouse Beach** and **Eve's Beach**, are more crowded and lively. Lighthouse Beach is far and away the most happening and has a long line of bars screening pirated Hollywood films, cafés selling muesli and pastries and hawkers peddling crafts or drugs.

Further south still is where the classy resorts are clustered. **Pulinkudi Beach** and **Chowara Beach**, respectively 8 km and 10 km to the south, is where to go for hand-and-foot attentiveness, isolation, heritage-style villas and Ayurveda in luxurious surrounds. Chowara Beach has security staff but some sunbathers still feel plagued by hawkers.

Poovar Island

Poovar Island, 20 km south, has several resorts on the landward side of a lagoon, with access to the beach (where you will be bombarded by local fisherkids demanding cash, pens and the shirt off your back) by motorboat. There are now lifeguard patrols but you still need to be careful when swimming. Kovalam's stretch of the Arabian Sea can get rough, particularly between April and October, with strong riptides and swells of up to 6 m. From May the sea level rises, removing the beach completely in places, and swimming becomes very dangerous.

Vizhinjam

Within easy walking distance of Kovalam, sandwiched in between Lighthouse and Poovar beaches but scarcely visited by tourists, is Vizhinjam, a scruffy town with a low-rise string of bangle shops, banana stalls, beauticians and seamstresses sewing jasmine buds onto strings for garlands. It's hard to believe it today but Vizhinjam was once the capital of the Ay rulers who dominated South Travancore in the ninth century AD. In the seventh century they had faced constant pressure from the Pandiyans who kept the Ay chieftains under firm control for long periods. There are rock-cut sculptures in the 18th-century **cave temple** here, including a rough sculpture of Vinandhara Dakshinamurthi in the shrine and unfinished

Kovalam

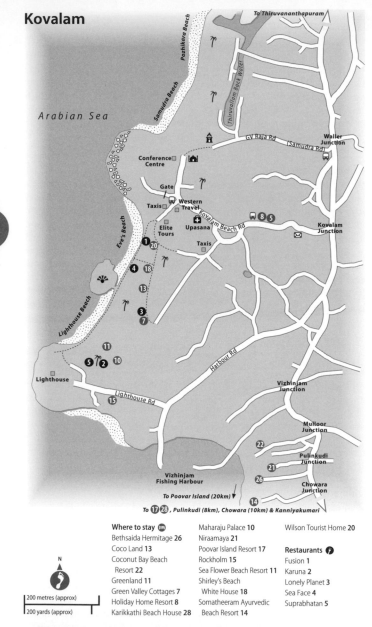

Arabian Sea

To Thiruvananthapuram

Pozhikkara Beach

Samudra Beach

Thiruvallam Back Water

GV Raja Rd

Waller Junction

(Samudra Rd)

Conference Centre

Gate

Taxis

Western Travel

Eve's Beach

Elite Tours

Upasana

Kovalam Beach Rd

Kovalam Junction

Taxis

Lighthouse Beach

Harbour Rd

Lighthouse

Lighthouse Rd

Vizhinjam Junction

Mulloor Junction

Pulinkudi Junction

Vizhinjam Fishing Harbour

Chowara Junction

To Poovar Island (20km)

To 17 28 , Pulinkudi (8km), Chowara (10km) & Kanniyakumari

N

200 metres (approx)
200 yards (approx)

Where to stay
Bethsaida Hermitage **26**
Coco Land **13**
Coconut Bay Beach
  Resort **22**
Greenland **11**
Green Valley Cottages **7**
Holiday Home Resort **8**
Karikkathi Beach House **28**

Maharaju Palace **10**
Niraamaya **21**
Poovar Island Resort **17**
Rockholm **15**
Sea Flower Beach Resort **11**
Shirley's Beach
  White House **18**
Somatheeram Ayurvedic
  Beach Resort **14**

Wilson Tourist Home **20**

Restaurants
Fusion **1**
Karuna **2**
Lonely Planet **3**
Sea Face **4**
Suprabhatan **5**

42·Kerala Thiruvananthapuram & the far south

reliefs of Siva and Parvati on the outer wall. Today Vizhinjam is the centre of the fishing industry and is being developed as a major container port. The traditional boats are rapidly being modernized and the catch is sold all over India, but you can still see the keen interest in the sale of fish, and women taking headloads off to local markets.

Around Kovalam

South of Kovalam in Tamil Nadu is **Padmanabhapuram** ① *Tue-Sun 0900-1700 (last tickets 1600), Rs 200, child Rs 50 (accredited guide included, but 'donation' expected after the tour), camera Rs 25, video Rs 1500; best at 0900 before coach parties arrive, see page 46,* the old wooden palace of the Rajas of Travancore. Enclosed within a cyclopean stone wall, the palace served as the capital of Travancore from 1490-1790, and is a beautiful example of the Kerala school of architecture, with fine murals, floral carvings and black granite floors. It makes a great day trip, or a neat stopover if you're heading across the Tamil Nadu border to Kanniyakumari.

Listings Kovalam and nearby resorts *map p42*

Where to stay

Kovalam

Long power cuts are common here, so a/c often doesn't work. Look for rooms with windows on 2 walls to get a good through-breeze. There are numerous budget cottages and rooms to let with a range of rooms from Rs 150-1000. The alleys behind **Lighthouse Beach** tend to have the cheapest accommodation. Scouts greet arrivals at the bus stand but you may pay considerably more if you use their services. You will find rooms to let, behind bars and restaurants, by walking from the **Sea Rock Hotel** towards the lighthouse, and on the **Samudra Beach** and **GV Raja Rd** (Samudra Rd). Be aware that management of the cheaper hotels often changes hands and hotel names can change from year to year. Rates shown here are for the high season. Prices skyrocket in all hotels for the 3-week peak period (23 Dec-7 Jan), though it still pays to bargain. High season is 1-19 Dec, 11 Jan-28 Feb; in the low season, especially May-Jul, expect 40-75% discounts.

$$$$ Karikkathi Beach House
Near Nagar Bhagavathy Temple at Mulloor Thottam, Pulinkudi, T0471-272 0238, www.karikkathibeachhouse.com.
2 doubles with linked lounge, palm-thatched roof, no a/c or TV, perfect for honeymooners or those used to being kept; the house comes with private beach, chef, waiter and servants. There's a cottage should families or groups need extra beds.

$$$$-$$$ Niraamaya
Pulinkudi, near Kovalam, T0471-226 7333, www.niraamaya.in.
Sitting high on a rocky bluff between Kovalam and Kannyukumari, this elite resort boasts a world-class spa and offers Ayurveda treatments. There are just 21 traditional Keralite cottages, with 4-posters, big plantation chairs and open-air bathrooms, spread over 9 ha of foresty gardens. Excellent Sivananda

yoga on a one-on-one basis at an open-air pavilion overlooking the sea.

$$$$-$$$ Poovar Island Resort
Poovar Island, T0471-221 2068,
www.poovarislandresort.com.
Award-winning boutique hotel with 'floating' cottages where the backwaters meet the sea. Facilities include pool, handicrafts, Ayurveda, watersports.

$$$$-$$$ Somatheeram Ayurvedic Beach Resort
Chowara Beach, south of Kovalam,
T0471-226 8101, www.somatheeram.in.
Kerala's first Ayurvedic resort, and one of its best, with cottages and traditional Keralite houses set in coconut groves dotted over a steep hill above the beach. 20 doctors and 90 therapists work in 5 treatment rooms and 24 massage rooms at the shared Ayurvedic facilities.

$$$$-$$ Bethsaida Hermitage
Pulinkudi, T0471-226 7554,
www.bethsaidahermitage.com.
Eco-friendly stone and bamboo beach *cabanas* surrounded by coconut groves. Profits support a variety of charitable projects. Family-friendly, informal and unpretentious.

$$$$-$$ Coconut Bay Beach Resort
Mulloor, T0471-234 3524,
www.coconutbay.com.
Spacious stone villas on beach, good restaurant, friendly. Secluded location in traditional fishing village. Recommended.

$$ Kailasam Yoga and Ayurveda Holidays
Kovalam, T0471-248 4018, book through
Free Spirit Travel, T+44 (0) 1362 683616
(UK), www.yogaindia.co.uk.
Peaceful oasis set up by a yoga teacher and Ayurvedic physician. Yoga classes

held in tiled areas under coconut-leaf roofs, surrounded by trees and open-sided to catch the sea breezes. Price includes all yoga classes.

$$ Maharaju Palace
Lighthouse Beach, T(0)9946-854270,
www.maharajupalace.com.
Beautiful, shady garden setting, quiet and set back from beach. 6 very clean rooms inside and outside cottages complete with chandeliers and frou-frou interiors. Genial staff, very popular.

$$ Rockholm
Lighthouse Rd, T0471-248 0406,
www.rockholm.com.
Very pleasant hotel owned by an Anglo-Indian family with cheerful staff. Good-sized rooms, with balcony, in a wonderful position just above the lighthouse. Direct access to beach. Good terrace restaurant.

$$-$ Coco Land
Between Lighthouse Beach and
Eve's Beach, T0471-248 1341,
www.cocolandheritage.com.
Bamboo huts and 'luxury' wood cottages in a little garden set back from the beach. Cottages boast TVs, a/c and hot water. Friendly management. Recommended.

$$-$ Holiday Home Resort
Beach Rd, T0471-248 0497,
www.holidayhomeresort.net.
Cute cottages amid a tree-filled, shady garden with hammocks to laze in. Serene location 10 mins' walk from beach. Excellent, friendly service from the helpful manager, Shar.

$$-$ Hotel Greenland
Lighthouse Beach, T0471-232 3485.
Friendly female manager has a variety of spotlessly clean rooms set amongst

her flowery garden. All have porch, fly-screens, 4 have kitchenettes and TV. Cheaper rooms are excellent value. Recommended.

$$-$ Shirley's Beach
Between Lighthouse Beach and Eve's Beach, T0471-231 7303, www.shirleysbeach.com.
The sea-facing rooms here are a cut above other hotels in this price range. All are breezy and painted a cheerful blue, some with balcony. The owner is a wealth of knowledge. Quiet location, very good value. Recommended.

$ Green Valley Cottages
Between Lighthouse Beach and Eve's Beach, T0471-248 0636.
Spick and span simple non-a/c rooms with fly-screens and sit-outs. Good value.

$ Sea Flower Beach Resort
Lighthouse Rd, T0471-248 0554, www.seaflowerkovalam.com.
Great location right on the shore. 5 good-sized rooms with decent bath and balcony. Helpful staff, good value, big discounts for long stays.

$ Wilson Tourist Home
Up path behind Neelakanta Hotel, T0471-248 0052. Rs 600-1200.
Clean, quiet rooms with bath, balcony, fan, some with a/c. Open-air restaurant, pretty garden, helpful service. Recommended.

Restaurants

Kovalam
There are hundreds of restaurants here. Service can be slow, and quality hit-and-miss since management often changes hands. Below is a very short list of those that have proved consistent. The restaurant at the **Taj** is good, if predictable. **The Leela** hotel Sun brunch has a giant salad counter and loud live music. Avoid 'catch of the day' on Sun – it's unlikely to be fresh. Some restaurants will screen pirated DVDs, sometimes to compensate for underwhelming cuisine.

$$ Fusion
Eve's Beach, T0471-248 4153.
Kovalam's take on fusion food doesn't really pull it off but the cold coffees are exceptional and the menu has a nice varied mix of international and Indian food.

$$ Rockholm Hotel
(See Where to stay), Lighthouse Rd.
Very good international food and tandooris served on a pleasant terrace with beautiful views, especially early morning.

$$ Sea Face
Eve's Beach, T0471-248 1835, www.seaface.com.
Breezy raised terrace on the beach by a pleasant pool. Varied choice including versatile fish and seafood. Friendly and attentive.

$ Karuna
Lighthouse Beach.
Excellent Keralite breakfasts, home-made brown bread, decent coffee.

$ Lonely Planet
Between Lighthouse Beach and Eve's Beach.
Wholesome, mildly spiced Ayurvedic vegetarian food. Set around a pond with ducks – and mosquitoes. Sells recipe books and runs cookery courses.

$ Suprabhatam
Lighthouse Beach, opposite Hotel Greenland.
South and North Indian vegetarian meals.

Entertainment

Kovalam
Kalakeli Kathakali Troupe, *T0471-248 1818*. Daily performances at many high-end hotels.

Shopping

Kovalam
Numerous craft shops, including Kashmiri and Tibetan shops, sell a wide range of goods. Most are clustered around the bus stand at the gate of the Ashok with another group to the south around the lighthouse. Good-quality paintings, metalwork, woodwork and carpets at reasonable prices. Gems and jewellery are widely available but it is notoriously difficult to be sure of quality. Tailoring is available at short notice and is very good value with the fabrics available. Tailors include: **Brother Tailors**, 2nd Beach Rd; **Raja**, near hotel Surya; and **Suresh**, next to Garzia restaurant.

Zangsty Gems, *Lighthouse Rd*. Sells jewellery and silver and has a good reputation for helpfulness and reliability.

What to do

Kovalam
Body and soul
Ayurvedic treatments are offered by most upmarket resorts, where a massage will set you back anything from Rs 700 to more than Rs 2000.
Dr Franklin's Panchakarma Institute and Research Centre, *Chowara, T0471-248 0870, www.dr-franklin.com*. The good doctor's family has practised Ayurveda for 4 centuries, and he himself is the former district medical officer of the Keralan government. Programmes include treatment for infertility, sluggishness, paralysis and obesity.

15-day body purification therapy (*panchakarma* and *swetakarma*).
Medicus, *Lighthouse Rd, T0471-248 3710, www.ayurbay.com*. Mrs Babu has a loyal clientele, many of whom return year after year.
Padma Nair, *Pink Flowers, Lighthouse Beach, T(0)9895-882915, www.padma karma.com*. One of *Kalaripayattu* master Balachandran Nair's students, Padma Nair offers 1-week yoga holiday programmes at her village home from US$250.

Fishing
Can readily be arranged through the hotels, as can excursions on traditional catamarans or motor boats. You may be promised corals and beautiful fish just offshore but don't expect to see very much.

Indian martial arts
Guru Balachandran Nair, *is the master of the Indian School of Martial Arts, Parasuvykal, 20 km from Trivandrum, T0471-223 2686, www.kalari.in*. This is a college teaching *Kalaripayattu*, Kerala's traditional martial art, as well as *Kalarichikitsa*, an ancient Indian healing tradition combining Ayurveda with *Marma* therapy, which manipulates the vital pressure points of the body to ease pain. A fighter would have had an intimate knowledge of these points to know what to harm or how to heal. A fascinating place to stay.

Tour operators
There are dozens of tour operators on the roads leading down to the beach and on the beachfront. Nearly all of them offer money exchange, onward travel booking and backwater tours.

Great Indian Travel, *Lighthouse Rd,
T0471-248 0173, www.gitstour.com*.
Kerala Tours, *T0858-903 9767, www.
keralatours.com*. Wide range of tours,
exchange, packages to eco-friendly
beach resorts.
Visit India, *Lighthouse Rd, T0471-248
1069*. Friendly and helpful, exchange,
short backwater tours from Thiruvallam.

Transport

Kovalam

There are 3 main points of access to
Kovalam's beaches. Remember to
specify which you want when hiring
an auto or taxi.

Bus Local: Frequent buses
depart 0540-2100 to East Fort,
Thiruvananthapuram, from bus stand
outside **Ashok Hotel** gate on Kovalam
Beach (30 mins, Rs 9). From **East Fort
bus station**, walk or catch an auto-
rickshaw to town centre (Rs 20).
    Long distance: To **Kanniyakumari,
Kochi** via **Kollam** (**Quilon**) and **Kottayam,
Nagercoil, Padmanabhapuram,
Varkala** and **Thodopuzha** via **Kottayam**.

Rickshaw Auto-rickshaw to
Thiruvananthapuram, Rs 150-170,
but bargain hard.

Taxi From taxi stand or through
Ashok or **Samudra** hotels. One-way
to **Thiruvananthapuram** or airport,
around Rs 300; city sights Rs 1200-1400;
Kanniyakumari, Padmanabhapuram,
Rs 2800 (8 hrs); **Kochi**, Rs 4300 (5 hrs);
Kollam, Rs 2700; **Thekkady**, Rs 2700
(6 hrs). **Note** Fares estimated from
http://www.savaari.com.

Varkala

popular but low-key backpacker hangout in a dramatic cliff-top setting

Like Gokarna in Karnataka, Varkala (population 42,300) is a pilgrimage centre for both backpackers and Hindus. The former come for the ruddy beach which lies at the bottom of the dramatic drop of a laterite cliff, the latter for the Vaishnavite Janardhanaswamy Temple and the Sivagiri Mutt of social reformer Sree Narayana Guru.

Sights and beaches

The sea is far from calm (it has lifeguards for good reason), and the main beach, **Papanasam**, accessed by steep steps hacked in the cliffs, is shared between

Varkala

To **3**
4
Kairali Ayurudeic Yoga Centre
To Alimood Mosque
Scientific School of Yoga
To **1**, Edavai (3 km), Pallavur & Kollam (35 km)
Thiruvandadi Beach Rd
N

200 metres
200 yards

9 Keraleeyam (Massage/Yoga)
8

North Cliff

3
6

Doctor's Ayuruedic Health Centre
1
2

Appu's Store

Where to stay
Akshay Beach Resort **2**
Gateway **20**
Govt Guest House **7**
Hill View Beach Resort **9**
Marine Palace **5**
Mektoub **1**
Panchavadi **13**
Sea Pearl Chalets **18**
Sea Splendour **3**
Sunshine Home & Johnny
 Cool Restaurant **6**
Varkala Deshadan **8**
Villa Jacaranda **16**

6
Taxis
Helipad
Laundry
Kerala Kathakali Centre

Cliff Rd

Papanasam Beach

Nature Cure Hospital
Suresh Handicrafts
Mineral Springs
Book Exchange

5

Restaurants
Caffé Italiano **1**
Clafouti **4**
Funky Art cafe **3**
Juice Shack **2**
Oottupura **5**
Sri Padman **8**

18
13
7
20

South Cliff

Elegance of India, Master Crafts
2
Beach Rd

Sri Rama Hanuman
Tank
8

16
Vaishanvaite Janardhanaswamy
Temple Junction

To Railway station (2½ km), Sivagiri (3½ km) & Thiruvanenpuram (50 km)

holidaymakers and fishermen. Watch your step around the cliff, particularly at night; carry a torch after dark.

Along the cliff path, particularly along the **North Cliff**, is the tourist village high street; sizeable concrete hotels, travel agents, internet cafés, tailors stitching out endless pairs of fisherman's trousers and a huge preponderance of Kashmiri and Tibetan salespeople pushing their customary turquoise, silverware and carpets.

Further north, the tourist shacks bleed into fishing village life around the **Alimood Mosque** (dress modestly).

The south, bordered by a golden beach, has a lovely village feel, with traditional houses built around the 13th-century temple dedicated to Vishnu. The **Arratu festival** in March-April draws thousands of visitors.

Opposite is the **Sri Rama Hanuman Temple**, whose large temple tank three-wheeler drivers splash through in the morning, while women thwack their *lungis* clean on its steps. The main 'town' area (including the train station) is a further 2 km inland from Temple Junction.

Golden Island

A two-hour excursion takes you to Golden Island for a glimpse of local backwaters; there's a small temple here but it's the type of visit you'd make for the atmosphere more than anything else. A boat round the island should cost Rs 50 for the hour.

Listings Varkala map p48

Where to stay

There are at least 50 guesthouses, plus rooms in private houses. The North Cliff area is compact, so look around until you find what you want: the northernmost area is where the most laid-back, budget options are and has the most character, while the far south side has a few fancier places. None, however, is actually on the beach. Outside the high season of Nov-Mar, prices drop by up to 50%. During the monsoon (Jun-Jul) many close.

$$$ Villa Jacaranda
Temple Rd West, South Cliff, T0470-261 0296, www.villa-jacaranda.biz.
A delightful guesthouse home, with 5 huge rooms elegantly but sparely decorated. Jasmine, birds of paradise and magnolia blossoms are tucked into alcoves, there's a lotus-filled pond and tropical garden and everything is immaculately maintained. Guests have their own keys and entrance. Really special.

$$$-$$ Mektoub
Odayam Beach, T(0)9447-971239.
13 non a/c rooms in a beautiful rustic-mystic hideaway – a place of candles and incense smoke. Charming owner, utterly peaceful, and a minute from uncrowded sand.

$$$-$ Hill View Beach Resort
North Cliff, T0470-260 5744, www.varkalahillview.com.
Self-contained cottages and budget rooms in a smart resort. Internet, airport pick-up, hot water.

$$ Varkala Deshadan
*Kurakkanni Cliff, T0470-320 4242,
www.deshadancliffbeachresort.com.*
Scrupulously clean Chettinadu-style a/c
bungalows set around a large pool. Price
includes breakfast.

$$-$ Akshay Beach Resort
*Beach Rd (about 200 m from beach),
T0470-260 2668.*
Wide variety of bright, clean rooms.
Quiet location away from the cliff.
Restaurant, TV lounge, good value.

$$-$ Marine Palace
*Papanasam Beach, T0471-260 3204,
www.varkalamarine.com.*
18 rooms in total with 3 lovely old-style
wooden rooms with balconies and a
sea view. The honeymoon suite has a
truly gigantic bed. Good service and
nice tandoori restaurant on the beach.
Recommended.

$$-$ Sea Pearl Chalets
*Beach Rd, T0470-260 0105,
www.seapearlchalets.com.*
Circular thatched huts perched scarily
near the cliff edge. Great views, breakfast
included. Recommended.

$ Government Guest House
*Towards The Gateway (see
Restaurants), T0470-260 2227, www.
dtpcthiruvananthapuram.com.*
Immense, high-ceilinged rooms with
marble floors and big baths, in the
leafy former summer residence of the
maharaja. Isolated, idyllic and quiet.
Book in advance, recommended.

$ Panchavadi
*Beach Rd, T0470-260 0200,
www.panchavadi.com.*
Excellent location close to beach.
24 Very clean and secure with simple

rooms. Budget rooms very good value.
Restaurant, helpful staff. Recommended.

$ Sea Splendour
*North Cliff end, Odayam Beach, T0470-
266 2120, www.seasplendour.com.*
Homely choice with simple rooms in
retired teacher's guesthouse. Excellent
home-cooking (unlimited and spoilt for
choice), very peaceful.

$ Sunshine Home/Johnny Cool &
Soulfood Café
*North Cliff, Varkala Beach,
T(0)9341-201295.*
Colourful, chilled-out Rasta house set
back off the cliff. Bongo drums and
Marley posters abound. There's a variety
of rooms, some with balcony, plus a little
standalone thatched cottage out the
back. The café does pastas, noodles, fish
and chips – but in its own sweet time.

Restaurants

There are numerous restaurants along
North Cliff, most with facsimile menus,
slow service and questionable kitchens;
take extra care with drinking water
here. 'Catch of the day' splayed out for
you to inspect, usually costs Rs 100-150
depending upon the type/size of fish,
but make sure you don't get 'catch of
yesterday' (fresh fish keep their glassy
eyes and bright silvery scales). Many
restaurants close out of season.

$$$ The Gateway
*Gateway Hotel, near Government
Guest House.*
Every day 1230-1500. Includes pool use.
Good-value eat-all-you-want buffet,
delicious rich vegetarian cuisine.

$$ Caffé Italiano
North Cliff, T(0)9846-053194.
Good Italian and seafood, but quite pricey.

$$ Sri Padman
Near Hanuman Temple, T0472-260 5422.
Sri Padman's terrace overlooking the temple tank offers the best non-beachfront position in town. Come here for South Indian vegetarian breakfasts served in big stainless steel *thali* trays, and oily *parathas* to sop up spicy curries and coconut chutneys.

$ Clafouti
Clafouti Hotel, North Cliff (see Where to stay).
Fresh pastries and cakes, but standards seem to drop when the French-Keralite owners are away.

$ Funky Art Café
North Cliff.
Eclectic multi-cuisine menu. Sometimes hosts local bands playing Varkala versions of Western rock songs, which can be an amusing diversion while waiting for the incredibly slow service.

$ The Juice Shack
Cliffside Varkala, turn off at Tibetan market, T(0)9995-214515.
Shady little spot with healthy juice, good coffee and excellent toasted sandwiches. Brilliant for breakfast – even has Marmite.

$ Oottupura
Cliffside Varkala, near helipad, T0472-260 6994.
A Varkala institution. Excellent 100% vegetarian with 60 curries and everything from Chinese to macaroni cheese. Breakfast can be *iddlies* or toasted sandwiches, all served under a giant pistachio tree covered in fairy lights.

Entertainment

Varkala is a good place to hang out, chill and do yoga but there's no organized nightlife to speak of, only impromptu campfire parties.

Kerala Kathakali Centre, *by the helipad, T0470-2603612.* Holds a daily *Kathakali* demonstration (Rs 150, make-up 1700-1800, performance 1830-2000). The participants are generally students of the art rather than masters.

Shopping

Most of the handicraft shops are run by Kashmiris, who will tell you that everything (including the tie-dye T-shirts) is an antique from Ladakh.

Elegance of India and **Mushtaq**, *Beach Rd.* Sell Kashmiri handicrafts, carpets, jewellery, etc, reported as honest, will safely air-freight carpets and other goods.
Satori, *T(0)9387-653261.* Cliff-top boutique, selling pretty Western clothes made with local fabric and jewelled Rajasthani slippers.
Suresh, *on path south from helipad.* Handicrafts from Karnataka.

What to do

Body and soul
Keraleeyam, *North Cliff.* One of the best of the many yoga/Ayurvedic massage centres.
Lakshmi Herbal Beauty Parlour, *Clafouti Hotel (see Where to stay).* Individual attention, amazing massages plus waxing, henna, etc.
Nature Cure Hospital, *North Cliff.* Opened in 1983, treats patients entirely by diet and natural cures including hydrotherapy, chromotherapy (natural sunbath with different filters) and mud

therapy, each treatment normally lasting 30 mins.

Naturomission Yoga Ashram, *near the helipad*. Runs 1-, 2- and 7-day courses in yoga, massage, meditation, and healing techniques. Payment by donation.

Scientific School of Yoga, Naturopathy and Massage, *Diana Inn, North Cliff, T0470-320 6294*. 10-day yoga and massage course (2 classes daily), Rs 500, professionally run by English-speaking doctor. Also has a shop selling Ayurvedic oils, soaps, etc.

Tour operators

Most hotels offer tours, air tickets, backwater trips, houseboats, etc, as do the many agents along North Cliff.
JK Tours & Travels, *Temple Junction Varkala, T0802-668 3334. Daily 0900-2100*. Money exchange.
Lullaby@Varkala, *www.lullabyatvarkala. in*. Runs tours of the local sites, and also introduce tourists to *anganwadis*, childcare centres for underprivileged families. The project helps feed, clothe and educate its beneficiaries.

Bus To/from **Temple Junction** (not beach) for **Alappuzha** and **Kollam**, but often quicker to go to Paripally on NH47 and catch onward buses from there.

Motorcycle Kovalam Motorcycle **Hire**, Voyager Travels, Eye's Beach Rd, T0471-248 1993. Next door to **JA Tourist Home**, Temple Junction; and **Mamma Chompo**, Beach Rd.

Rickshaw/taxi Autos and taxis can be found on Beach Rd and near the helipad. Both charge about Rs 50 to train station. Taxi to **Thiruvananthapuram**, Rs 1000 (1¼ hrs).

Train Varkala sits on the Kochi–Trivandrum line, with at least 20 trains a day in each direction. All northbound trains call at **Kollam**, while many of the south-bound trains continue to **Kanniyakumari**.

Backwaters

★ Kerala is synonymous with its lyrical backwaters: a watery cat's cradle of endlessly intersecting rivers, streams, lagoons and tanks that flood the alluvial plain between the Indian Ocean and Western Ghats. They run all the way from Kollam via Alappuzha and Kottayam to Kochi to open up a charming slow-tempo window onto Keralite waterfront life: this is the state's lush and fertile Christian belt, Arundhati Roy country, with lakes fringed by bird sanctuaries, idyllic little hamlets, beside huge paddy ponds rustling in the breeze.

The silent daybreak is best, as boats cut through the mist, geese and ducks start to stir along banks, plumes from breakfast fires drift out across the lagoons. As the hamlets and villages wake, Kerala's domestic scene comes to life: clothes are pounded clean, teeth brushed, and smartly turned out primary school children swing their ways to class.

Luxury houseboats are the quintessential way of seeing the waterfront, but they can be shocking polluters, and if your budget or attention span won't stretch that far the state-operated ferries will give you much the same access for a fraction of the fee. Alternatively, borrow a bicycle or move around by car; both the roads and canals thread their way through flood plains the size of football pitches, brown lakes with new shoots prodding out and netted fields that protect prawns and fish from snooping white egrets.

Essential Backwaters

The chief embarkation point for houseboat trips through the backwaters is Alappuzha (Alleppey), 64 km south of Kochi on the shore of Lake Vembanad. Trains pull in at the station 3 km west of the town centre, while the bus stand is right on the waterfront, a short walk from several budget hotels and the main houseboat jetty. The other main centres are Kumarakom, across the lake from Alappuzha and a short taxi ride from the railway station at Kottayam; and Kollam, 70 km north of Trivandrum on the southern end of Lake Ashtamudi, linked to Alappuzha by road, rail and ferry.

Best places for a splurge

Purity, **Alappuzha**, page 61
Marari Beach, **Alappuzha**, page 61
Raheem Residency, **Alappuzha**, page 62
Coconut Lagoon, **Kumarakom**, page 67

Getting around

Houseboats
Alappuzha is the starting point of backwater boat trips to Kollam, Changanacherry, Kottayam and Kochi, and everybody you meet seems to have a houseboat to rent. Some find cruising the backwaters of Lake Vembanad utterly idyllic and restful, while for others the sluggish pace of the houseboats – combined with the heavy crowding of the waterways close to Alappuzha – a form of slow torture. Most first-time visitors go for an overnight tour, which is in some ways the worst of all worlds: you're often moored alongside a raft of other boats, you get trotted through the standard tourist 'village' visits

Tip...
A cheap alternative to a houseboat is to spend a few hours riding the ferries that ply across Lake Vembanad and south to Kollam. The 'tourist boat' from Alappuzha to Kollam gives you eight hours on the water at a bargain price of Rs 300, but it's a long day and lacks the peace of the best houseboats.

(ie shopping trips), and you simply don't have time to get away from the crowds. If you can spare an extra night or more, longer cruises let you get away into the deeper reaches of the backwaters where canal life still continues more or less unmolested by tourism. On the other hand, if you just want a taste of the scenery, a day cruise – or even one of the cheap ferries that ply the lakes and canals – might satisfy you at a fraction of the price of a night on a houseboat.

Other transport
Buses, trains and taxis link the main backwaters towns, but the most appealing ways to explore are by bike and boat. For details, see Transport, page 59.

Time required

Allow at least two days for a houseboat tour if you want to get away from the crowds and experience the deeper backwaters which are less affected by tourism. Day tours are a cheaper alternative for those short on time who want to enjoy some backwater scenery.

Best cheap places to stay
Government Guest House, **Kollam**, page 58
Palmy's Residency, **Alappuzha**, page 63

Kerala backwaters

To Kodungallur

Kochi (Cochin)
Ernakulam
Aroor
Vembanad Lake
5
NH47
Vayalar Lake
1
Cherthala
Vembanad Lake
Vechoor
Mararikulam
Kannangarapally
Kadthuruthi
4
8
2
Pathiramanal
Muhamma
Manganam
Kumarakom
Vembanad Lake
Ettumanoor
Chithira
Kottayam
R Block
3
6
Alappuzha (Alleppey)
7
Moncombu
Kumarankari
Nedumudi
Champakulam
Changanacherry
Kidangara
Karumadi
Edathna
Neepettupuram
9
Mannarsala
Nagaraja
Thottappally
Temple
Haripad
Chengannur
Thrikkunnapuzha
Mavelikara
Azheekal
Kayambkulam
Ayiramthengu
Ochira
NH47
Vallikkavu
10
Arabian Sea
Karungappally
N
Chavara
Munroe Island
Ashtamudi Lake
5 km
5 miles
Kollam (Quilon)
Ashramam

Kollam (population 361,400) is a busy shaded market town on the side of the Ashtamudi Lake and the headquarters of India's cashew nut trading and processing industry. It is congested and there's little reason to linger, but its position at the south end of Kerala's backwaters, where the waterways are less crowded than those further north, make it a good alternative starting point for boat trips up the canals. See What to do, page 58.

Known to Marco Polo as 'Koilum', the port saw trading between Phoenicians, Persians, Greeks, Romans and Arabs as well as the Chinese. Kollam became the capital of the Venad Kingdom in the ninth century. The educated king Raja Udaya Marthanda Varma convened a special council at Kollam to introduce a new era. After extensive astronomical calculations the new era was established to start on 15 August AD 825. The town was associated with the early history of Christianity.

From the KSWTC boat jetty in the city centre you can hire houseboats or sightseeing boats (a houseboat in appearance but with large seating areas instead of bedrooms) to explore the palm-fringed banks of **Ashtamudi Lake**. You might see Chinese fishing nets and large-sailed dugouts carrying the local crops of coir, copra and

Where to stay 🛏
Anthraper Home Stay **1**
Coconut Palms **9**
Emerald Isle
  Heritage Villa **7**
Keraleeyan Lakeside
  Ayurvedic Resort **3**
Marari Beach &
  Marari Beach Home **4**

Mata Amritanandamayi
  Ashram **10**
Olavipe **5**
Pooppally's Heritage
  Homestay **6**
Purity **2**
Vembanad House
  Homestay **8**

ON THE ROAD
Preserving the backwaters for the future

The backwaters are lagoons fed by a network of perennial rivers with only two permanent outlets to the sea. The salts are flushed out between May and September, but sea waters rush inland by up to 20 km at the end of the monsoon and the waters become increasingly brackish through the dry season. This alternation between fresh and salt water has been essential to the backwaters' aquatic life. However, as land value has rocketed and reclamation for agriculture has reduced the surface water area, the backwaters' fragile ecology has been put at risk. Many of the original swamps have been destroyed and the waters are becoming increasingly saline.

Tourism, too, is taking its toll. Exploring the backwaters in a traditional *kettuvallam* is the ultimate Kerala experience but the popularity of these trips is having an adverse effect on the waterways. However, there are ways to help prevent further degeneration.

The trend so far has been for houseboat operators to offer larger, more luxurious boats (some even equipped with plunge pools) to meet the demands of tourists. The powerful outboard motors contribute heavily to pollution levels in the canals. Opting for a smaller boat not only helps ease environmental damage but also allows you to venture into the many narrower and less visited lagoons that the larger boats are unable to access.

Some operators are becoming aware of the damage being caused and are putting responsible travel practices in place. Support these efforts by checking that your houseboat is equipped with a chemical toilet (to prevent your waste being dumped into the canals) and, if possible, opting for a solar-powered boat. Alternatively consider hiring a hand-propelled *thoni* or canoe as an entirely carbon neutral way of exploring this unique region.

cashew. **Munroe Island** is a popular destination for tours, with coir factories, good birdwatching and narrow canals to explore.

Kollam to Alappuzha
Mata Amritanandamayi Ashram ① *10 km north of Kollam at Vallikkavua, accessible by boat or road (through Kayambkulam or Karungappally), www.amritapuri.org, Rs 150 per day.* This giant, pink skyscraper sandwiched on the backwaters between the sea and the river, is the ashram of 'Amma' (the hugging 'Mother'). Thousands of people, Western and Indian alike, attend *Darshan* in hope of a hug. The ashram feels a bit lacklustre when Amma is on tour. She has hugged around three million people so far. In the early days, these used to last for minutes; now she averages one hug every 1½ seconds, so she can happily hug 30,000 in a day. The ashram has shops, a bank, library and internet. Smoking, sex and alcohol are forbidden.

Mannarsala Some 32 km before Alappuzha, Mannarsala has a tremendously atmospheric **Nagaraja Temple** buried deep in a dense jungle forest. Traditionally *naga* (serpent) worshippers had temples in serpent groves. Mannarsala is the largest of these in Kerala with '30,000 images' of snake gods lined up along the path and among the trees, and many snakes living around the temple. Childless women come for special blessing and also return for a 'thanksgiving' ceremony afterwards when the child born to the couple is placed on special scales and gifts in kind equalling the weight are donated. The temple is unusual for its chief priestess.

Haripad and around The village of **Haripad** has one of Kerala's oldest and most important Subrahmanya temples. The four-armed idol is believed to have been found in a river, and in August the three-day **Snake Boat Race** at **Payipad**, 3 km by bus, commemorates its rescue and subsequent building of the temple. There are boat processions on the first two days followed by competitive races on the third day. There is a guesthouse on **Mankotta Island** on the backwaters; the large comfortable rooms with bath are well kept.

Thottapally Squeezed between the backwaters and the sea, and 12 km from Haripad station, Thottapally makes a good stop on a backwaters trip, two hours from Alappuzha.

Aranmula About 10 km from Chengannur, Aranmula has the **Parthasarathi Temple** and is known for its unique metal mirrors. The **Vallamkali** (or **Utthrittathi**) **festival** on the last day of Onam (August-September) is celebrated with a boat race. The festival celebrates the crossing of the river by Krishna, who is believed to be in all the boats simultaneously, so the challenge is to arrive at the same time, rather than race.

Listings Kollam (Quilon) and around *map p55*

Tourist information

Kollam

District Tourism Promotion Council (DTPC)
Govt Guest House Complex, T0474-275 0170; also at DTPC bus station, T0474-274 5625, train station and ferry jetty, www.dtpckollam.com.
Offers cruises, coach tours, and details of Kathakali performances.

Where to stay

Kollam

$$$$-$$$ Aquaserenne
Paravoor, 15 mins from town by road or boat, T0474-251 2410.
Splendid backwaters location, well-furnished chalets (some reassembled Kerala houses) with TV, restaurant, Ayurvedic massage/treatment, boat rides.

$$$$-$$$ Fragrant Nature Retreat and Resorts
Paravur, T0474-251 4000,
www.fragrantnature.com.
A 4-star luxury lakeside resort with spa, swimming pool and jacuzzi. Accommodation in lakeside rooms or villas.

$$ Nani
Opposite clock tower, Chinnakada,
T0474-275 1141, www.hotelnani.com.
Swish business hotel close to the railway station, with smart if slightly overpriced rooms and friendly staff.

$ Government Guest House
Ashramam, T0474-274 2838.
Live like the British Raj on a pauper's budget. 12 simply furnished rooms, all with attached bath, in the sprawling former residence of the British governor. More expensive rooms have bathrooms large enough to throw a party in. High ceilings, shady veranda, huge garden, bags of character, friendly staff. Some cheaper rooms are in bland modern building at the back. Meals on request. Recommended.

$ Tamarind (KTDC)
Ashramam, T0474-274 5538,
www.ktdc.com.
Newly renovated rooms in a bland block building. All rooms with a/c, TV. Nice views of the waterway. Quiet location, restaurant, boat hire.

Kollam to Alappuzha

$$-$ Coconut Palms
Kumarakodi, T0471-301 8100,
www.coconutpalms.co.in.
Idyllic 200-year-old traditional house in shaded compound, on backwaters and 100 m from sea. Yoga, Ayurveda and package deals available.

$ Mata Amritanandamayi Ashram
Vallikkavu, T0476-289 6399,
www.amritapuri.org.
Amma's ashram offers spartan but spacious accommodation in a multi-storey block, with hugs and South Indian meals included in the price. Western canteen (at extra cost) serves American-style meals.

Restaurants

Kollam

$ Eat N Pack
Near Taluk Office, Main St.
Excellent value, clean, good choice of dishes, friendly. Recommended.

$ Indian Coffee House
Main Rd.
For good coffee and vegetarian and non-vegetarian South Indian food. Nice waiter service and good atmosphere.

$ Suprabhatam
Opposite clock tower, Main St.
Adequate vegetarian.

Festivals

Kollam
Jan Kerala Tourism Boat Race.
Apr Colourful 10-day **Vishnu festival** in Asram Temple with procession and fireworks.
Aug-Sep Avadayattukotta Temple celebrates a 5-day **Ashtami Rohani** festival. **Muharram** too is observed with processions at the town mosque.

What to do

Kollam
Cruises and boat trips
As well as houseboat trips on traditional *kettuvallams*, there are also the much cheaper options of Kollam–Alappuzha

cruises and shorter canal journeys to Munroe Island. The gentle pace and tranquil waterways make these tours very worthwhile, but the heat and humidity may sometimes make overnight stays on houseboats uncomfortable.

DTPC (see Tourist information, above). Offers daily 8-hr backwater cruise from Kollam to Alappuzha; depart 1030 (Rs 300). You can be dropped off halfway at Alumkadavu (Rs 200) or at Vallikkavu for the Ashram (Rs 150). The only stops are for meals; some travellers find the trip a little too long and samey. A good alternative is a canal trip to Munroe Island village; depart 0900, 1300 (6 hrs return, Rs 500).

A more expensive option is to hire a *kettuvallam*. For a 1-bed houseboat prices start at Rs 5000 for overnight, ranging up to Rs 14000 for 2 days and 1 night, inclusive of all meals. There are also cruise packages which combine a day cruise with an overnight stay at a backwater resort (Rs 3500).

Southern Backwaters Tour Operators, *opposite KRSTC Bus Station, Jetty Rd, Kollam, T(0)9495-976037, www.southern backwaters.com.* Independent operators. A/c deluxe and standard houseboats for 1- to 3-night packages. Also motorboat cruises and Munroe Island tours.

Transport

Kollam
Local auto-rickshaws are plentiful and bikes are available for hire.

Bus Local buses are plentiful. Long-distance buses run from the KSRTC station, T0474-275 2008. Buses every 30 mins from 0600 to **Kochi** (3½ hrs) via **Alappuzha** (2 hrs) and other towns on the coast. Buses run 24 hrs to **Thiruvananthapuram**, leaving every 10 mins in the day and every 30 mins during the night (2 hrs). Change at Thiruvananthapuram for **Kovalam**. It is difficult to get to **Varkala** by bus; take the train.

Car To **Alappuzha**, Rs 2000, from the bus station.

Ferry Public ferries sail to **Ghuhandapuram** at 0730, 1100, 1330, 1545 and 1745 (1 hr, Rs 5) and then return to Kollam. It's an interesting journey with views of village life and Chinese fishing nets on the way. The 1745 departure lets you enjoy sunset over the waterways. See also Backwater cruises under Tour operators, above.

Train Junction railway station, T131, is about 3 km east of the boat jetty and bus station. There are several trains a day south to **Thiruvananthapuram** including the *Island Exp 16526*, 1335 (1¾ hrs), which continues to **Kanniyakumari** (4¼ hrs). All the trains stop at **Varkala** (½ hr).

An equal number of trains head north to **Ernakulam** (**Cochin**) and points beyond, including the *TVC Chennai Exp 12696* (continues to **Chennai**, 15 hrs); and the *Island Exp 16525* (continues to **Bengaluru**, 16 hrs).

Alappuzha (Alleppey) and around

ramshackle town with thousands of houseboats and a vast network of waterways

Alappuzha (pronounced *Alappoorra;* population 177,100) has a large network of canals, choked with the blue flowers of water hyacinth, passing through the town. It's the chief departure point for cruises into the backwaters and the venue for the spectacular snake boat races (see Festivals, page 64). Houseboat trips can be arranged at any of the numerous tour operators in town or directly, by heading to the boat dock just off VCNB Road. Although the town itself doesn't have many tourist sites, it's a pleasant, bustling place to walk around and there's a lovely stretch of undeveloped beach as well.

Mararikulam

On the coast, 15 km north of Alappuzha, Maraikulam is a quiet, secluded beach which, until recently, was only known to the adjoining fishing village. The main village has a thriving cottage industry of coir and jute weaving.

Alappuzha (Alleppey)

Where to stay	Palmy's Residency 3	Himalaya Bakery 9
Cherukara Nest 1	Raheem Residency &	Hot Kitchen 1
Govt (KTC) Guest House 6	Chakara Restaurant 14	Indian Coffee House 3
Johnson's The Nest 13	St George Lodge 5	Komala 4
Keraleeyam Lake Side		Saurashtra 5
Ayurvedic Health	**Restaurants**	
Resort 9	Alleppey Prince 7	
Motty's Homestay 11	Harbour 8	

N

200 metres
200 yards

Champakulam and around

Some 16 km southeast of Alappuzha is the hushed backwaters village of **Champakulam** where the only noise pollution is the odd squeak of a bicycle and the slush of a canoe paddle. The Syrian Christian church of St Mary's Forane was built in 1870 on the site of a previous church dating from AD 427. The English-speaking priest is happy to show visitors round. Nearby the St Thomas Statuary makes wooden statues of Christ for export round the world: a 2-m-tall Jesus will set you back US$450. To get there, take the Alappuzha–Changanacherry bus (every 30 minutes) to Moncombu (Rs 4), then an auto-rickshaw to Champakulam (4 km, Rs 12). Alternatively the Alappuzha–Edathna ferry leaves at 0615 and 1715 and stops at Champakulam. In the backwater village of **Edathna**, you can visit the early Syrian St George's Church.

Listings Alappuzha (Alleppey) and around *map p60*

Tourist information

ATDC
Komala Rd, Alappuzha, T0477-226 4462, www.atdcalleppey.com.

DTPC
KSRTC bus station near jetty, Alappuzha, T0477-225 3308. Open 0830-2000.
Helpful and offers good backwaters trips.

KTDCI
Motel Araam, Alappuzha, T0477-224 4460.

Where to stay

Book ahead to avoid the scramble off the ferry. Hotels north of Vadai Canal are quieter.

$$$$ Olavipe
Thekanatt Parayil, Olavipe, T0478-252 2255, www.olavipe.com.
Century-old mansion belonging to family of Syrian Christian notables, on a 16-ha organic farm on the lush island of Olavipe. 6 rooms: 4 in the main house and 2 in a cottage.

$$$$ Purity
Muhamma, Aryakkara (8 km from Alappuzha town), T0484-221 6666, www.malabarhouse.com.
This beautiful Italianate villa, set on an acre of tropical grounds overlooking Lake Vembanad, is the most elegant lodging for miles around, with minimalist decor and a smattering of rare antiques. Huge rooms on the ground floor open out to a grassy lawn, but for the ultimate splurge check in to the huge turquoise-toned suite upstairs, with arched windows hoovering up views of the glassy lake. There's a pool and a discreet spa offering Ayurvedic treatments and yoga classes, and high-class dinners, which the chef can tailor to your wishes, are served around a pond in the courtyard. Superb in every respect and thoroughly recommended.

$$$$-$$$ Marari Beach
Mararikulam, Alappuzha, T0478-286 3801, www.cghearth.com.
Well-furnished, comfortable, local-style cottages (garden villas, garden pool villas and 3 deluxe pool villas) in palm groves – some with private pool. Good

seafood, pool, Ayurvedic treatment, yoga in the morning, *pranayama* in the evening, shop, bikes, badminton, beach volleyball, boat cruises (including overnight houseboat), farm tours, friendly staff, discounts Apr-Sep. Recommended.

$$$ Anthraper Home Stay
Cherthala, T0478-281 3211, www.anthrapergardens.com.
Charming country house on the backwaters. Sprawling garden, cooking demonstrations, yoga, canoeing, fishing and river walks.

$$$ Emerald Isle Heritage Villa
Kanjooparambil–Manimalathan, T0477-270 3899.
5 rooms on the shores of an island of lush jungle, surrounded by sunken paddy field. Toddy on tap, cookery courses, boat trips, Ayurveda. The magic of the place begins on the 10-km journey from Alappuzha.

$$$ Motty's Homestay
Kidangamparambu Rd, Alappuzha, T(0)9847-032836, www. mararibeachhomes.com.
Just 2 double rooms, with old furniture and 4-poster beds, in a private house on Alappuzha's outskirts. Excellent home-cooked breakfast and dinner included.

$$$ Raheem Residency
Beach Rd, Alappuzha, T0477-223 9767, www.raheemresidency.com.
Special luxury heritage hotel housed in a beautifully restored colonial 19th-century bungalow, on a pristine piece of Kerala's coast. 10 immaculate rooms, all with a/c and lovely antique furnishings. Palatial living room, jasmine-scented garden, excellent restaurant and a lovely pool under a velvet apple tree. The Irish journalist owner also offers the property as a writers' retreat (contact for prices). Easily the best address in Alappuzha. Recommended.

$$$ Vembanad House Homestay
Puthankayal, Alappuzha, T0478-286 8696, www.vembanadhouse.com.
4 spacious rooms in stately heritage house surrounded by a lake in the pretty Muhamma area. Fresh food from the family farm cooked to Kerala recipes. Traditional architecture with modern bathrooms (no a/c). The house is managed by the delightful Balakrishnan family.

$$$-$$ Pooppally's Heritage Homestay
Pooppally Junction, Nedumudy, T0477-276 2034, www.pooppallys.com.
Traditional wooden cottage (water bungalow) and rooms, with open-air bathrooms, in 19th-century family farmhouse, shaded by a mango tree, set in a garden stretching down to the River Pampa. Great home-cooked food. Catch the ferry to Alappuzha for 90 mins of free houseboat.

$$ Keraleeyam Lakeside Ayurvedic Health Resort
Off Thathampally main road, Alappuzha, T0477-223 7161, www.keraleeyam.com.
Keraleeyam sits on one of the prettiest nubs of the backwaters and is one of the most reasonable places to embark on a proper Ayurvedic programme. Doctors attend daily, there's no alcohol, and the menu is tailored according to your Ayurvedic body type. Cottages on the lake are better than the drab rooms in the main house.

$$-$ Cherukara Nest
Just around the corner from KSRTC bus station, Alappuzha, T0477-225 1509, www.cherukaranest.com.
Airy, cool, spotlessly clean rooms in a peaceful traditional family home. Rattan furniture on large shady porches. Pigeon house in the back garden. Very helpful and friendly. Meals available on request.

$ Johnson's The Nest
Lal Bagh Factory Ward (west of Convent Sq), Alappuzha, T0477-224 5825, www.johnsonskerala.com.
Friendly family-run guesthouse in a quiet street away from the town centre. 6 rooms, each with balcony. Free pick-up from bus station, internet, houseboat facility, popular.

$ Palmy's Residency
North of new Matha footbridge, Alappuzha, T0477-223 5938, www.palmyresidency.com.
Large, clean rooms with fly-screens and fans. Quiet but central location. More expensive rooms have big balconies to lounge in. Local waterway canoe trips (4-5 hrs, Rs 500 per hr). Free bike hire. Recommended.

$ St George Lodge
CCNB Rd, Alappuzha, T0477-225 1620.
Don't let the dilapidated façade put you off – this is an excellent cheapie. 80 very basic but clean rooms, some with attached bath. Friendly staff.

$ Tamarind (KTDC)
Jetty Rd, Alappuzha, T0477-224 4460, www.ktdc.com.
Bright yellow building next door to the KSRTC bus station. More expensive rooms are large but have tired-looking bathrooms. Cheaper bamboo-walled rooms on 3rd floor. Free bike hire, internet.

Restaurants

$$$ Chakara
Raheem Residency, Beach Rd.
Rooftop dining with attentive service and excellent multi-cuisine food. The 4-course set dinner menu (pegged at rupee equivalent to €11) is unbeatable value. Alcohol available.

$$ Alleppey Prince Hotel
AS Rd (NH47), 2 km from town.
International, comfortable a/c restaurant, reasonable food, alcohol in bar only.

$ Harbour
Beach Rd.
Specializes in seafood, also has Indian and European dishes. Excellent value. Alcohol available.

$ Himalaya Bakery
SDV Rd.
Large range of sweet and savoury pastries, and other snacks, to take out or eat in at the tiny seating area.

$ Hot Kitchen
Mullakal Main Rd.
Good for *iddli, dosa, vadai*, etc.

$ Indian Coffee House
Mullakal Main Rd.
Good value, tasty non-vegetarian snacks.

$ Komala
Komala Hotel, Zilla Court Ward.
Excellent South Indian *thalis* and Chinese.

$ SAS
Jetty Rd.
Good South Indian vegetarian and Chinese.

$ Saurashtra
Cullan Rd.
Vegetarian, ample helpings on banana leaf, locally popular.

Festivals

9-12 Jan Cheruppu is celebrated in the Mullakkal Devi Temple with a procession of elephants, music and fireworks.
17-19 Jan Tourism Boat Race.
Jul/Aug DTPC Boat Race (3rd Sat) in the backwaters. **Champakulam Boat Race**, Kerala's oldest, takes place 16-km ferry ride away on 'Moolam' day. The **Nehru Trophy Snake Boat Race**, www.nehrutrophy.com/htm/boat. htm, inaugurated in 1952, is the largest snake boat race in the state. As many as 40 highly decorated 'snake boats' are rowed by several dozen oarsmen before huge crowds. Naval helicopters do mock rescue operations and stunt flying. Entry by ticket; Rs 50-2000 depending on viewing class. There are other snake boat races held throughout the year.

What to do

Houseboat cruises
It's always worth booking in advance during high season, when the theoretical government-set rates (which are printed and displayed in the DTPC booking office at the jetty in Alappuzha) go out the window, and houseboat owners jack the prices up by 50-80%. Houseboats vary widely depending on the number of bedrooms, facilities (some come with a/c, flatscreen TVs and DVD players), quality of food and the crew's level of English. Booking ahead gives you some degree of certainty over the level of luxury you will find; it also allows you to circumvent the persistent dockside touts, whose commissions mean that any discount you can negotiate comes at the cost of corners cut on the trip. If you're coming outside peak season, and don't mind spending a morning scouting around, making a

booking on the spot gives you a chance to inspect a number of boats before agreeing on a price.

The following companies are generally at the top end of the market, but offer reliably good (in some cases superb) service.
CGH Earth, *T0484-301 1711, Kochi, www. cghearth.com*. Runs 'spice boat' cruises in modified *kettuvallams*, which are idyllic if not luxurious: shaded sit-outs, modern facilities including solar panels for electricity, 2 double rooms, limited menu. US$325.
Discovery 1, *Malabar House, Fort Kochi, see page 76*. **Malabar Escapes'** take on the houseboat goes against the grain by being silent,pollutant free, and bright turquoise. Because it's nimble and trips are for a minimum of 3 nights, it's guaranteed to take you far from the wider watery motorways bigger rice boats ply. 1 bedroom, large bathroom and sitting room plus sun deck. Food is to Malabar House's high standard.
DTPC, *Jetty Rd, T0477-225 1796, www. dtpcalappuzha.com*. Runs the same 8-hr backwater cruises as its sister office in Kollam, only in reverse. Departs 1030 from Alappuzha ferry jetty (Rs 300). There is also a shorter round-trip to Kumarakom (4 hrs, Rs 150), and canoe trips through local waterways (Rs 200 per hr).
Lakes and Lagoons Tour Co, *Punnamada, T0477-226 6842, www.lakeslagoons.com*. Solar-powered boats with up to 3 bedrooms. Consistently recommended operator.
Rainbow Cruises, *Mamood Junction opposite jetty, Alappuzha, T0477-223 1110, www.rainbowcruises.in*. Solar powered with high safety standards and emergency speedboat support (houseboats have been known to sink).

Transport

It is only a 5-min walk between the ferry jetty and the KSRTC bus station despite what many local rickshaw drivers will tell you.

Bus From the **KSRTC Bus Station**, T0477-225 2501, there are frequent long-distance buses to **Kochi**, 0630-2330 (1½ hrs); **Thiruvananthapuram**, 0600-2000 (4 hrs) via **Kollam** (2 hrs); **Champakulam**, 0515-2000 (45 mins) and **Kottayam**, 0730-1800 (1½ hrs). There are several buses daily to **Coimbatore**, from 0600 (7 hrs).

Car A car with driver from Alappuzha to **Fort Kochi** (65 km) costs Rs 500-600.

Ferry Public ferries sail from the Boat Jetty T0477-225 2015, swtd.kerala.gov.in, to **Kottayam**, 0730, 0935, 1130, 1430 and 1715 (3 hrs), and **Changanassery**, 1300 and 1645, 3 hrs). Also frequent services to **Nedumudi** (1 hr).

Train The train station, T0477-225 3965, is on the coastal route from **Trivandrum–Varkala–Kollam–Ernakulam**, 3 km from the jetty. Frequent trains in both directions.

Around Kottayam lies some of the lushest and most beautiful scenery in the state, with hills to its east and backwaters to its west.

Kottayam

Kottayam itself (population 60,700) is the capital of Kerala's Christian community, which belonged to the Orthodox Syrian tradition up till the Portuguese arrival. Two churches of the era survive 2 km north of town, in the 450-year-old **Cheria Palli** ('Small' St Mary's Church), which has beautiful vegetable dye mural paintings over its altar, and the **Valia Palli** ('Big' St Mary's Church), from 1550, with two Nestorian crosses carved on plaques behind two side altars. One has a Pallavi inscription on it, the other a Syriac. The cross on the left of the altar is the original and may be the oldest Christian artefact in India; the one to the right is a copy. By the altar there is an unusual small triptych of an Indian St George slaying a dragon. Note the interesting Visitors' Book (1898-1935); a paper cutting reports that "the church has attracted many European and native gentlemen of high position". Mass at Valia Palli at 0900 on Sunday, and Cheria Palli at 0730 on Sunday and Wednesday. The Malankara Syrian Church has its headquarters at Devalokam.

Ettumanoor

Just north of Kottayam, Ettumanoor has possibly the wealthiest temple in Kerala. The present Mahadeva temple was constructed in 1542, and is famous for its murals depicting scenes from the *Ramayana* and the Krishna legends, both inside and outside the *gopuram*. The typical circular shrine with a copper-covered conical roof encloses a square sanctuary. The **Arattu festival** in March draws thousands of pilgrims when gold elephant statues are displayed. They weigh 13 kg each.

Kumarakom and Vembanad Lake

Tucked among the waterways of Vembanad Lake, in mangrove, paddy and coconut groves with lily-studded shores, is **Kumarakom**, 16 km from Kottayam. Here are stacks of exclusive hotels where you can be buffed and Ayurvedically preened, bent into yoga postures, peacefully sunbathe or take to the water: perfect honeymoon territory.

The tourism department has developed an old rubber plantation set around Vembanad Lake into a **bird sanctuary** ① *1000-1800*. A path goes through the swamp to the main bird nesting area. **Pathiramanal** ('midnight sands') **Island** in the middle of the lake can be reached by boat. The best season for birdlife is June-August; visit in the early morning.

Tourist information

DTPC
*Government Guest House, Nattakom,
Kottayam, T0481-256 0479,
www.dtpckottayam.com.*

Responsible Tourism Travel Desk
T0481-252 4343, Kumarakom.
Books tours to meet local craftsmen.

Where to stay

In Kumarakom 26% taxes are added
to bills.

Kottayam

$$$$ Philipkutty's Farm
*Pallivathukal, Ambika Market,
Vechoor, T0482-927 6530,
www.philipkuttysfarm.com.*
5 immaculate waterfront villas sharing
an island on Vembanad Lake. The
delightful working farm boasts coconut,
banana, nutmeg, coca and vanilla
groves. Delicious home-cooking and
personal attention from all the family.
No TV. Cooking and painting holidays.

$$ Aida
*MC Rd, 2 km from railway, T0481-256
8391, www.hotelaidakerala.com.*
Rs 2100 (plus taxes) Clean, pleasant
rooms with bath, some with a/c. Front
rooms can be noisy. Restaurant, bar,
helpful staff.

$$-$ Anjali Park
*KK Rd, 4 km from railway, Kottayam, T0481-
256 3661, www.hotelanjalipark.com.*
Decent rooms with bath and a/c.
Good restaurants.

$ Ambassador Hotel
KK Rd (set back), T0481-256 3293.
Friendly Indian-style hotel with good
restaurant and bar. Very good value.

$ Kaycee's Residency
Off YMCA Rd, Kottayam, T0481-256 3440.
Good value, clean, decent-sized rooms.

$ PWD Rest House
*On a hill 2 km south of Kottayam,
T0481-256 8147.*
Remarkable late 19th-century building
with superb furniture, overlooking vista
of paddy fields.

Kumarakom

$$$$ Privacy at Sanctuary Bay
*Kannamkara, opposite Kumarakom,
T0484-221 6666, www.malabarhouse.com.*
Absolute lakeside isolation in a fully
staffed but fully self-contained
3-bedroom bungalow. Modern opulent
interiors hide behind the old Keralite
façade, and there's a stunning veranda
looking out across the lake.

$$$$-$$$ Coconut Lagoon (CGH Earth)
*Vembanad Lake, T0481-252 5834,
www.cghearth.com.*
Comfortable heritage *tharavads*
(traditional Keralite wooden cottages),
heritage mansions and pool villas.
Outdoor restaurant facing lagoon,
good dinner buffet, pool, yoga, very
friendly, Ayurvedic treatments, attractive
waterside location, spectacular approach
by boat (10 mins from road). Vechoor

cows mow the lawns. Discounts Apr-Sep. Recommended.

$$$-$$ Waterscapes (KTDC)
T0481-252 5861, www.
waterscapeskumarakom.com.
Idyllic cottage experience on the backwaters. All chalets have a/c and cable TV. Pool, bar, restaurant.

$$ GK's Riverview Homestay
Valliadu, Aymanam, T0481-259 7527,
www.gkhomestay-kumarakom.com.
Set amid paddy fields in the heart of *God of Small Things* country, George and Dai's lovely house offers home comforts in the shape of simple immaculate rooms, hammocks lazily overlooking the river, and superb Kerala cooking. The consummate hosts are always on hand to share secrets of the area, and arrange excellent tours.

Restaurants

Kottayam

$$ Aida
MC Rd.
Large, uninspired menu. Pleasantly cool 'chilled' drinks may arrive slightly warm.

Kumarakom

$$$ Baker's House (Vivanta by Taj)
Kumarakom, T0481-252 5711.
One of Kerala's most atmospheric restaurants, the Baker's House (as featured in *The God of Small Things*) is magic at dusk, when brass lamps twinkle all around the 120-year-old bungalow. Expect to pay for pan-global high-end cuisine, but stick to the Kerala seafood for best results.

Transport

Kottayam
Bus The new **Private Bus Station** is near the railway station. Buses to Alappuzha only leave from the **KSRTC Bus Station**, 2 km away; local buses to **Kumarakom Tourist Village** also run frequently from here. There are fast and frequent long-distance buses to **Alappuzha**, every 45 mins (2 hrs); **Thiruvananthapuram**, every 30 mins (4 hrs); **Kochi**, every 30 mins (1½ hrs) and **Kumily**, every hour (4½ hrs). There are 2 evening departures to **Madurai**, 2045 and 2145 (7 hrs) and 5 buses daily head to **Munnar**, 0600-1600 (5 hrs).

Car Car with driver to **Thekkady**, Rs 1400, 4 hrs.

Ferry Ferries leave from the **Kodimatha Jetty** except during the monsoons, when you should head to the **Town Jetty** 3 km southwest of the train station. Ferries to **Alappuzha**, 0730, 0930, 1130, 1430, 1730 (3 hrs). This is an interesting trip but gets very busy in peak season. Other departures include **Champakulam**, 1530 (4 hrs) and **Mannar**, 1430 (3 hrs).

Train Trains run throughout the day, south to **Thiruvananthapuram** via **Kollam** and **Varkala**, and north to Ernakulam and beyond. No trains to Alappuzha, which is on the parallel coastal line.

Fort Kochi
& Ernakulam

Charming Fort Kochi (Cochin) is a true one-off in modern Kerala: a layer cake of colonial India, where British parade grounds overlay Portuguese forts, where Dutch palaces slowly crumble into the soil alongside synagogues, where every turn takes you down some romantically fossilized narrow winding street. Despite a tourist invasion that's flooded the lanes with antique shops, internet cafés and shops flogging fisherman trousers, parts of the ramshackle island still feel frozen back in the 15th and 16th centuries, and the huge trees here are so old that their parasitic aphids are as tall as trees themselves.

In the southern quarter of Mattancherry, row upon row of wood-fronted doors give glimpses of rice and spice merchants sitting sifting their produce into small 'tasting' bowls. The iconic batwing Chinese fishing nets, first used in the 14th century, stand on the shores of the north fort area, silhouetted against the lapping waters of one of the world's finest natural harbours.

Before arriving in Fort Kochi, however, you have to negotiate the city's modern centre of gravity – grubby, dynamic Ernakulam, a Rs 5 ferry ride and half a world away across the harbour. While Fort Kochi languishes dreamily in the past, its ambitious sibling is expanding outwards and upwards at breakneck pace, propelled by the vast new container terminal on Vallarpadam Island.

Essential Fort Kochi and Ernakulam

Finding your feet

Kochi's mellow little international airport is at Nedumbassery, 36 km northeast of the city centre. The smoothest way into town is to arrange a pick-up from your hotel (Rs 900-1500 depending on type of car and what your hosts feel the market will support). Alternatively, hire a prepaid taxi from the booth after Customs; a transfer to Fort Kochi costs around Rs 800, a little less to downtown Ernakulam. Air-conditioned buses leave the airport for Fort Kochi bus stand, right in the centre next to the Chinese fishing nets, between 0500 and 1900, taking 90 minutes.

Most trains pull into Ernakulam Junction station in the busy city centre. State-run long-distance buses arrive at the Central Bus Stand, 500 m north of Ernakulam Junction, while private buses pull in to the terminal at Kaloor Junction about 2 km further north. Local buses, taxis and auto-rickshaws connect the various transport hubs. A rickshaw from either to the main jetty, for Fort Kochi, costs approximately Rs 25. For details, see Transport, page 83.

Best Fort Kochi hotels

Malabar House, page 76
Brunton Boatyard, page 76
Old Courtyard, page 77
Caza Maria Hotel, page 78

Fact...

The first port in India capable of handling the huge container ships that until now have had to berth in Colombo or Singapore, Kochi stands poised to transform India's logistical landscape, and over the next decade this hitherto sleepy southern city will undoubtedly assume a front-and-centre seat in the future of the Indian economy.

Getting around

Fort Kochi has all the sights and a huge number of hotels, and many visitors never leave its cosy bubble. The quiet roads are easy to explore on foot or by bicycle, with an occasional cameo from an auto-rickshaw. If you need to get across to Ernakulam there are two routes: a circuitous trip by bus, taxi or auto-rickshaw (Rs 250-500), or one of the cheap and cheerful ferries that chug across the harbour to Ernakulam's Main Jetty – an enjoyably breezy 30-minute trip that's most atmospheric around sunset (ferries run 0600-2130). From the jetty you can catch a rickshaw to the railway station or bus stand for around Rs 40. Leave plenty of spare time if you need to travel during peak hours. After 2130 public transport begins to grind to a halt and you'll need to take a rickshaw or taxi to get around.

Vasco da Gama Square and around

If you land at the Customs Jetty, a plaque in nearby Vasco da Gama Square commemorates the landing of Vasco da Gama in 1500. Next to it is the **Stromberg Bastion**, "one of the seven bastions of Fort Emanuel built in 1767", named after the Portuguese king. Little is left of the 1503 Portuguese fort except ruins. Along the seafront, between the Fort Kochi Bus Stand, the boat jetty and the Dutch cemetery, run the cantilevered Chinese fishing nets. These are not unique to Kochi, but are perhaps uniquely accessible to the short-stay visitor.

St Francis' Church and around

Fort Kochi, Mon-Sat 0930-1730, Sun afternoon, Sun services in English 0800 (except for the 3rd Sun of each month).

Originally dedicated to Santo Antonio, the patron saint of Portugal, St Francis is the first church to reflect the new and European-influenced tradition. The original wooden structure (circa 1510) was replaced by the present stone building (there is no authority for the widely quoted date of 1546). Vasco da Gama died on the site in 1524 and was originally buried in the cemetery. Some 14 years later his body was removed to Portugal. The church was renamed St Francis in 1663, and the Dutch both converted it to a Protestant church and substantially modified it. They retained control until 1795, adding the impressive gable façade at the entrance. In 1804, it became an Anglican church. In 1949 the congregation joined the Church of South India. Note the old string-pulled *punkahs* (fans) and the Dutch and Portuguese gravestones that now line the walls.

Near St Francis' Church, Santa Cruz Cathedral was originally built in 1557 by the Portuguese, and used as a warehouse by the British in the 18th century, was rebuilt in the early 20th century. It has lovely carved wooden panels and pulpit, and an interesting graveyard.

Mattancherry Palace and Parikshith Thampuran Museum

Mattancherry, daily 1000-1700 except Fri and national holidays, Rs 2, photography not allowed.

The palace was first built by the Portuguese around 1557 as a sweetener for the Raja Veera Kerala Varma of Kochi bestowing them trading rights. In 1663, it was largely rebuilt by the new trading power, the Dutch. The layout follows the traditional Kerala pattern known as *nalukettus*, meaning four buildings, which are set around a quadrangle with a temple. There are display cases of the Rajas of Kochi's clothes, palanquins, etc, but these are no match for the amazing murals. The royal bedroom's low wooden walls squeeze the whole narrative of the *Ramayana* into about 45 16th-century panels. Every inch is covered with rich red, yellow, black and white. To the south of the Coronation Hall, the *kovinithilam* (staircase room) has six large 18th-century murals including the coronation of Rama. Vishnu is in a room to the north. Two of the women's bedrooms downstairs have

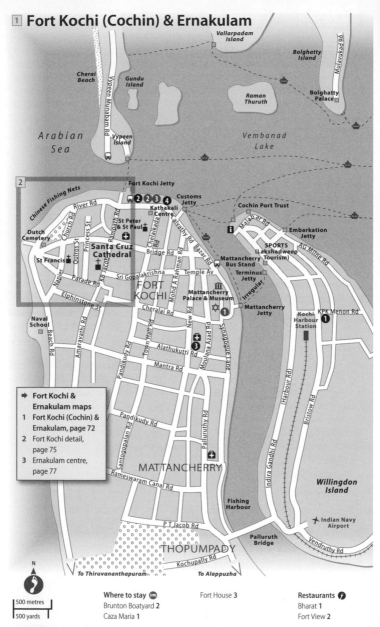

1 Fort Kochi (Cochin) & Ernakulam

Vallarpadam Island

Bolghatty Island

Mulavukad Rd

Cherai Beach

Gundu Island

Vypeen Munabam Rd

Bolghatty Palace

Raman Thuruth

Arabian Sea

Vypeen Island

Vembanad Lake

Chinese Fishing Nets

Fort Kochi Jetty

2 3 4 Customs Jetty

Kathakali Centre

River Rd

Church Rd

Ramnath Rd

Princess St

Chelakkada

Alvathy Rd

Bazar Rd

Cochin Port Trust

Malabar Rd

Embarkation Jetty

Dutch Cemetery

St Peter & St Paul

Santa Cruz Cathedral

Quiros St

Bridge Rd

Sri Gopalakrishna

Mohd A Rahman Rd

Temple Av

Mattancherry Bus Stand

SPORTS (Lakshadweep) Tourism

AG Milne Rd

St Francis

Napier

Parade Rd

FORT KOCHI

Mattancherry Palace & Museum

Terminus Jetty

Elphinstone St

Cheralai Rd

New Rd

Irregular

Mattancherry Jetty

KPK Menon Rd

Naval School

Beach Rd

Amaravathi Rd

Town Hall Rd

Alathukutti Rd

Moulana Azad Rd

Synagogue Lane

3

Kochi Harbour Station

1

Harbour Rd

Bristow Rd

Pandikudy Rd

Mantra Rd

Indira Gandhi Rd

Willingdon Island

Pandikudy Rd

Santoorapparan

Palluruthy Rd

Vendruthy Rd

MATTANCHERRY

Rameswaram Canal Rd

Fishing Harbour

Indian Navy Airport

P T Jacob Rd

Palluruth Bridge

THOPUMPADY

Kochupally Rd

To Thiruvananthapuram

To Alappuzha

→ **Fort Kochi & Ernakulam maps**
1 Fort Kochi (Cochin) & Ernakulam, page 72
2 Fort Kochi detail, page 75
3 Ernakulam centre, page 77

N

500 metres
500 yards

Where to stay	Fort House 3	Restaurants
Brunton Boatyard 2		Bharat 1
Caza Maria 1		Fort View 2

19th-century murals with greater detail. They relate Kalidasa's *Kumarasambava* and themes from the *Puranas*. If you are of a sensitive disposition avert your eyes from panel 27 and 29, whose deer, birds and other animals are captioned as giving themselves up to 'merry enjoyment', a coy way of describing the furious copulation and multiple penetration in plain view. Krishna, meanwhile, finally works out why he was given so many limbs, much to the evident satisfaction of the gopis who are looking on.

Synagogue

Mattancherry, Sun-Fri 1000-1200, 1500-1700, no video cameras, shoes must be removed.

Dating from 1568 (rebuilt in 1662), the synagogue is near Mattancherry Palace at the heart of what is known as Jew Town, which is a fascinating mixture of shops (some selling antiques), warehouses and spice auction rooms. Stepping inside the synagogue is an extraordinary experience of light and airiness, partly due to the 18th-century blue Cantonese ceramic tiles, hand painted and each one different, covering the floor. There are original glass oil lamps. For several centuries there were two Jewish communities. The earlier group (often referred to as 'black' Jews), according to one source, settled here as early as 587 BC. The earliest evidence of their presence is a copper inscription dated AD 388 by the Prince of Malabar. Those referred to as 'white' Jews came much later, when, with Dutch and then British patronage, they played a major role as trading agents. Speaking fluent Malayalam, they made excellent go-betweens

Fort Kochi

"If China is where you make your money," declared Italian traveller Nicolas Conti in the Middle Ages, "then Kochi surely is the place to spend it". Kochi has acted as a trading port since at least Roman times, and was a link in the main trade route between Europe and China. From 1795 until India's Independence the long outer sand spit, with its narrow beach leading to the wide bay inland, was under British political control. The inner harbour was in Kochi State, while most of the hinterland was in the separate state of Travancore. The division of political authority delayed development of the harbour facilities until 1920-1923, when the approach channel was dredged so ships that could get through the Suez Canal could dock here, opening the harbour to modern shipping. The current population is around 2.1 million.

for foreigners seeking to establish contacts. The community has shrunk to six families, with many now settled at Moshav Nevatim in Israel's Negev desert. The second Jewish synagogue (in Ernakulam) is deserted.

Ernakulam and around

East of Fort Kochi, Ernakulam has the **Museum of Kerala History** ① *1000-1200 and 1400-1600 except Mon and national holidays*. The museum exhibits start with Neolithic man and run through St Thomas and Vasco da Gama. Historical personalities of Kerala are represented with sound and light. Northwest of Ernakulam, **Bolghatty Island** has the 'palace' (circa 1745), set in large gardens and converted into a hotel. It was originally built by the Dutch and then became the home of the British Resident at the court of the Raja of Kochi after 1799. There is still some atmosphere of colonial decay which haunted the old building in its pre-modernized form and gave it much of its charm.

Vypeen Island lies on the northwestern fringe of the harbour. There are quiet beaches here, along with the Portuguese Azhikotta Fort, built around 1503. You can see cannon holes on the walls of the octagonal fort, which was garrisoned by 20 soldiers when it guarded the entrance to the backwaters. Vehicle ferries make the crossing from Fort Kochi.

Our Lady's Convent ① *Palluruthy, Thoppampady, 14 km south, by appointment, T0484-223 0508,* specializes in high-quality needlework lace and embroidery. The sisters are very welcoming and it is an interesting tour with items for sale.

Raksha ① *Yasmin Manzil, VII/370 Darragh-es-Salaam Rd, Kochangadi, T0484-222 7707,* works with children with physical and mental disabilities. Interested volunteers should contact the principal.

Hill Palace Archaeological Museum ① *Thirpunithura, 12 km east of Ernakulam, Tue-Sun 0900-1230, 1400-1700, Rs 11,* has a huge number of historical records and artefacts of the old royal state of Cochin, with portraits, ornaments, porcelain, palm leaf records and ancient musical instruments.

Kalady

Some 45 km northeast of Kochi is the town of Kalady, on the bank of the Periyar River. This popular pilgrimage site was the birthplace of one of India's most influential philosophers, **Sankaracharya**, who lived in the eighth century. He founded the school of *advaita* philosophy, which spread widely across South India. The **Adi Sankara Kirti Stambha Mandapam** ⓘ *0700-1900, small entry fee*, is a nine-storied octagonal tower, 46 m high, and details Sri Sankara's life and works and the Shan Maths, or six ways to worship. Inside the **Shankara Temple** (Hindus only), are two shrines, one dedicated to Sankaracharya and the other to the goddess Sarada. The management of the shrines is in the hands of the Math at Sringeri in Karnataka. Kalady can easily be visited in an afternoon from Kochi.

2 Fort Kochi detail

➡ Fort Kochi & Ernakulam maps
1 Fort Kochi (Cochin) & Ernakulam, page 72
2 Fort Kochi detail, page 75
3 Ernakulam centre, page 77

To Vypeen ▲

Chinese Fishing Nets
Fresh Fish Stalls
River Rd
Fort Kochi Bus Stand
Taxi
Children's Park
Vasco da Gama Square
Tower Rd
Dutch Cemetery
St Francis
Bastion Rd
Idiom Books
Cochin Club
Parade Ground
Fosse Rd
Santa Cruz Cathedral
Parade Rd
St Peter & Paul
Sanathana School of Yoga Studies
Napier St

N
200 metres
200 yards

Where to stay 🛏
Adam's Old Inn **1**
Delight Homestay **3**
Fort Muziris **2**
Koder House **6**
Malabar House & Restaurant **7**
Old Courtyard **8**

Old Harbour **13**
Oys Tourist Home **9**
Raintree Lodge **12**
Rossitta Wood Castle **11**
Trinity **5**
Vintage Inn **14**

Restaurants 🍴
Dal & Roti **1**
Kashi **2**
Marina **3**
Teapot Café **4**

Tourist information

Fort Kochi

Tourist Desk
Tower Rd, T0484-221 6129, www.
touristdesk.in. Open 0900-1800.
This travel agent, with good maps and
local information, runs daily backwater
tours, has information on more than
2000 temple festivals in Kerala, and
runs Costa Malabari guesthouse (see
page 121).

Ernakulam

Kerala Tourism Development
Corporation (KTDC)
Shanmugham Rd, T0484-235 3234.
Open 0800-1800.

Tourist Desk
Main Boat Jetty, Ernakulam, T0484-237
1761, see under Fort Kochi, above.

Where to stay

Fort Kochi
Fort Kochi has bags more character
than the busy commercial centre of
Ernakulam; book well in advance for
the Christmas period.

$$$$ Malabar House
1/268 Parade Rd, near St Francis' Church,
T0484-221 6666.
Fort Kochi's original boutique hotel, and
still one of its best. Big and beautiful
high-ceilinged rooms in a sensitively
restored 18th-century mansion, set
around a flagstone courtyard with an
excellent restaurant and small swimming
pool. Helpful staff, reliable airport pick-
ups and a funky bar make this a perfect
if pricey first place to hang your hat.

$$$$ Old Harbour
Tower Rd, T0484-221 8006,
www.oldharbourhotel.com.
Impeccably restored, 300-year-old
Portuguese and Dutch building slap on
the harbor front. Rooms have private
balconies, some with harbour views.
Large garden plus swimming pool,
Wi-Fi, Ayurveda, jacuzzi.

$$$$-$$$ Brunton Boatyard
Calvathy Rd, T0484-301 1711, www.
cghearth.com. Discounts Apr-Sep.
Easily the best address in Fort Kochi,
adjacent to the Chinese fishing nets
on the edge of the Arabian Sea.
18 characterful rooms and 4 deluxe
suites, each of which overlooks the
harbour in an elegantly restored original
boatyard and merchant's house built
around a courtyard with a giant rain-
tree. Generous swimming pool.

$$$ Koder House
Tower Rd, T0484-221 8485,
www.koderhouse.com.
Boutique hotel in a striking heritage town
house formerly owned by prominent
Jewish family, and sometime home to
ambassadors and heads of state. Luxury
suites have huge bedrooms, sitting room,
bathroom and jacuzzi. Tiny plunge pool
in the back courtyard, spa with massage
and facials, plus valet, business centre,
superb home-cooked food.

$$$-$$ Fort House
2/6A Calvathy Rd, T0484-221 7103,
www.hotelforthouse.com.
Tidy bungalows set in a quiet walled
courtyard with its own little jetty. Some
rooms charmingly old fashioned, others
made from bamboo. Newer, more
expensive rooms have modern baths,

but they're pretty spartan for the price. Good restaurant overlooking the water.

$$$-$$ Old Courtyard
1/371 Princess St, T0484-221 6302, www.oldcourtyard.com.

Beautiful, comfortable rooms, superbly styled with old wooden furniture, overlooking large, breezy courtyard of pretty pot plants and sit-outs. The suite is easily the most romantic with a 4-poster bed

③ Ernakulam centre

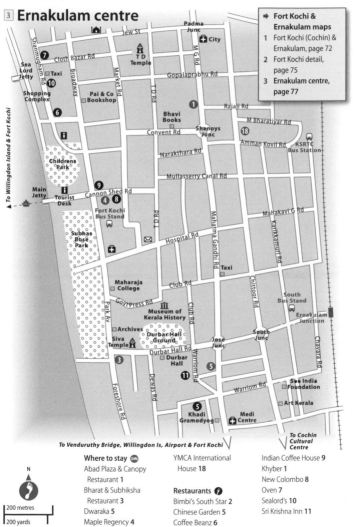

➡ Fort Kochi & Ernakulam maps
1 Fort Kochi (Cochin) & Ernakulam, page 72
2 Fort Kochi detail, page 75
3 Ernakulam centre, page 77

Where to stay
Abad Plaza & Canopy
    Restaurant **1**
Bharat & Subhiksha
    Restaurant **3**
Dwaraka **5**
Maple Regency **4**
YMCA International
    House **18**

Restaurants
Bimbi's South Star **2**
Chinese Garden **5**
Coffee Beanz **6**
Indian Coffee House **9**
Khyber **1**
New Colombo **8**
Oven **7**
Sealord's **10**
Sri Krishna Inn **11**

N
200 metres
200 yards

and white cotton. Attentive liveried staff, breakfast included, average food but excellent cakes and Turkish coffee, and lovely calm atmosphere. Recommended.

$$$-$ Rossitta Wood Castle
Rose St, T0484-221 5671,
www.hotelrossitta.com.
300-year-old Dutch mansion. Rooms, with quirky features and lots of wood-panelling, set around an open-air restaurant courtyard. Breakfast included. Art gallery, library internet café, spa, hot water, yoga.

$$ Caza Maria Hotel
6/125 Jew Town Rd, Mattancherry,
T(0)9846-050901, cazamaria1@gmail.com.
Just 2 huge and wonderful rooms in beautiful converted house, with tiled floors, wooden furniture and antiques: isolated (the only hotel in Jew Town), romantic and shabbily elegant. Fan only. All meals are included, served at French/Indian restaurant of same name across the street). Highly recommended.

$$ Delight Homestay
Parade Ground, Ridsdale Rd, T0484-221 7658, www.delightfulhomestay.com. Rs 2000-3500.
This lovingly restored Portuguese provides a welcoming peaceful haven. Airy, spotlessly 6 clean rooms open onto a wide terrace, budget rooms are great value. The garden is a riot of colourful blooms. Breakfast is served at the family table. A home away from home. Highly recommended.

$$ Raintree Lodge
Petercelli St, T0484-325 1489,
www.fortcochin.com.
Friendly little lodge in quiet location. Large clean rooms all with hot water and a/c. Pretty roof terrace to relax on.

$$-$ Fort Muziris
1/415 Burgar St, T0484-221 5057,
www.fortmuziris.com.
Friendly backpacker refuge in the centre of things. The pick of the rooms are the upstairs suites with kitchen and shared terrace.

$ Adam's Old Inn
CC1/430 Burgher St, T0484-221 7595,
www.adamsoldinn.com. Rs 750-1000.
Popular budget-traveller haunt in restored old building. Helpful manager.

$ Oy's Tourist Home
Burgher St, T(0)9947-594903,
www.oys.co.in. Rs 500-800.
Decent rooms in lovely lamp-lit old building, with lots of plants. Can be noisy.

$ Vintage Inn
Ridsdale Branch Rd, near Njaliparambu Junction, T0484-221 5064,
www.vintageresorts.in.
Wonderful, homely guesthouse with a cheerful owner. Airy modern rooms with huge baths in a quiet corner of town. Excellent value. Recommended.

Ernakulam

$$ Abad Plaza
MG Rd, T0484-238 1122, www. abadhotels.com. Rs 2900 (plus taxes).
A veteran of many monsoons, with large but slightly moth-eaten rooms all with a/c, fridge and cable TV. Rooms on street side can be noisy, quieter rooms on 5th floor. Breakfast included. Restaurants, gym, Ayurveda clinic, rooftop pool.

$$-$ Bharat
Gandhi Sq, Durbar Hall Rd, T0484-235 3501, http://bharathotel.com.
Popular business hotel. Clean spacious rooms, some a/c, best sea-facing. Restaurant with excellent lunch *thalis*

(South and North Indian). Great service, good value.

$$-$ Dwaraka
MG Rd, T0484-238 3236,
www.hoteldwaraka.com.
Centrally located, family-run hotel. Good-sized, rather noisy rooms with TV, some with balcony, excellent South Indian restaurant.

$$-$ YMCA International House
Chittoor Rd, 100 m from Central
Bus Station, T0484-238 3789,
www.ymcaernakulam.org.
Simple rooms (some a/c), restaurant, welcoming.

Fort Kochi
For a really fresh seafood meal, buy your own fish from the fishmonger stalls along the shorefront and take it to one of the nearby 'you buy, we cook' stalls, such as **Marina** or **Fort View**, where they'll be grilled or masala-fried with chips.

$$$ Malabar House Residency
See Where to stay.
Excellent seafood platter and chef's salad, the latter of huge dimensions. Authentic Mediterranean and local dishes.

$$ Caza Maria
Opposite the hotel, see Where to stay.
Open 1200-2130.
2 large rooms with wooden chairs, frescoes and old framed prints on the wall. Small menu includes fish *moilee* and lime rice, *palak paneer* and *chapatti* and apple pie and ice cream. Great atmosphere.

$ Dal Roti
1/293 Lilly St, T(0)974-6459244.
Firmly established favourite for pukka North Indian food – delicious *khati* rolls, huge stuffed *parathas* – served up by the affable Ramesh and his family. Don't arrive starving as queues often stretch out the door.

$ Kashi
Burgher St, Kochi, T0484-221 5769,
www.kashiartgallery.com.
If you've been away a while, **Kashi** is the type of place you'll fall on in wonder. The first 2 rooms are the art gallery, the rest is a restaurant where you can drink coffee fresh from your own cafetière, or indulge in a perfect cappuccino. There's a handful of excellently made sweets and 1-2 dishes they make for breakfast or lunch.

$ Kayikka's
Rahmathulla Hotel, Kayees, New Rd, near
Aanavaadal, Fort Kochi, T0484-222 6080.
Open 1200-1430, 1830-2030.
This family concern is the busiest biryani restaurant in Kochi and a local institution. Great mutton and chicken biryanis all week with fish biryanis on Fri and prawn on Tue. Arrive early to avoid disappointment.

$ Seagull
Calvathy Rd, T0484-221 7172,
www.thehotelseagull.com.
Good-value seafood, pleasant veranda for drinks and dining overlooking the harbour.

$ Teapot Café
Peter Celli St, T0484-221 8035.
Bare terracotta roof tiles dangle with teapots and fans, tables are tea crates and walls are hung with antique tea-related paraphernalia. Stop in for a brew of Darjeeling, Assam, Nilgiris or mint-flavoured teas, an iced coffee, or milkshake. There's a delicious selection of cakes and desserts, tasty toasted sandwiches and more substantial meals like prawn *moilee*, and mustard fish. With

loads of newspapers and magazines left out for customers to read, it's a lovely place to while away a couple of hours.

Ernakulam

$$ Bimbi's South Star
Shanmugam Rd.
Generous portions of tasty Indian food.

$$ Khyber
Durbar Hall Rd.
North Indian meals upstairs.

$$ Sealord's
Shanmugam Rd, T0484-238 2472, www.sealordhotels.com.
Rooftop setting with good fish and Chinese dishes.

$$ Sri Krishna Inn
Warriom Rd, next to Chinmaya Vidya Peeth, T0484-236 6664, www.sreekrishnainn.in.
One of the best pure-veg places in a city of seafood, with great North and South Indian options.

$$ Subhiksha
Bharat Hotel, see Where to stay.
Excellent value buffet lunch.

$ Bharat
Willingdon Island.
Very good vegetarian *thalis* and Indian specialities in clean surroundings.

$ Chinese Garden
Warriom Rd, T0484-236 3710.
Good variety of decent Chinese meals. Alcohol available.

$ Indian Coffee House
Cannon Shed Rd, T0484-322 3216, www.indiancoffeehouse.com.
Tasty North and South Indian dishes.

$ New Colombo
Canon Shed Rd.
Good snacks, fruit juices.

Cafés

Coffee Beanz
Shanmugan Rd, www.coffeebeanz.in. Daily 0900-2300.
Cold coffees, *appam*, *dosa*, popular, poky a/c coffee bar with just 6 tables.

Oven
Shanmugham Rd.
Good pizzas and snacks (savoury and sweet).

Entertainment

There are daily perfomances of *Kathakali*; see box, opposite. Arrive early to watch the extraordinary make-up being applied.

Fort Kochi
ENS Kalari, *Nettoor, T0484-270 0810, www.enskalari.org.in. Kalarippayattu* performances daily at 1915 (24 hrs' notice required).
Kerala Kathakali Centre, *River Rd, T0484-221 7552, www.kathakalicentre.com.* Rustic surroundings but lively performance, enjoyable; 1830-1930 (make-up 1700) but check timing, Rs 100.

Ernakulam
Cochin Cultural Centre, *Manikath Rd, off Ravipuram Rd, T0484-235 7153, www.cochin culturalcentre.com.* A/c 'theatre', authentic performance with English explanations; 1830-1930, make-up 1730, Rs 125.
See India Foundation, *Kalathil Parampil Lane (enter Chittoor Rd south) near Junction station, T0484-236 9471.* Dr Devan's 'interpreted' taste of *Kathakali* with esoteric English commentary; 1845-2000 (make-up from 1800), Rs 125.

Kathakali

The special dance form of Kerala, *Kathakali*, has its origins in the *Theyyam*, a ritual tribal dance of North Kerala, and *Kalaripayattu*, the martial arts practised by the high-caste Nayars, going back 1000 years. In its present form of dance-drama, *Kathakali* has evolved over the last 400 years.

The performance is usually outdoors, the stage bare but for a large bronze oil lamp, with the drummers on one side and the singers with cymbal and gong, who act as narrators, on the other. The art of mime reaches its peak in these highly stylized performances which used to last through the night; now they often take just three to four hours. The costume is comprised of a large billowing skirt, a padded jacket, some heavy ornaments and headgear. The make-up is all-important: *Pacha* (green) characterizing the good and *Kathi* (knife, shape of a painted 'moustache'), the Villain; *Thadi* (bearded), white for superhuman *hanuman*s, black for the hunter and red for evil and fierce demons; *Kari* (black) signifying demonesses; *Minukku* (shining) 'simple' make-up representing the gentle and spiritual. The paints are natural pigments while the stiff 'mask' is created with rice paste and lime. The final application of a flower seed in the lower eyelid results in the red eyes you will see on stage.

This classical dance requires lengthy, hard training to make the body supple, the eyes expressive. The 24 *mudras* express the nine emotions of serenity, wonder, kindness, love, valour, fear, contempt, loathing and anger. The gods and mortals play out their roles amid the chaos brought about by human ambition, but the dance ends in peace and harmony restored by the gods.

Festivals

Jan/Feb Ulsavam at the Siva Temple in Ernakulam for 8 days. Elephant processions each day, folk dance and music performances.
Aug/Sep Onam.
Nov/Dec Ulsavam at the Tripunithura Temple.

Shopping

Fort Kochi
Fort Kochi coir products (eg mats), carvings on rosewood and buffalo horn and antiques may catch your eye here. Several narrow streets in **Jew Town**, towards the synagogue, have become popular for 'antique' hunters in the last 25 years. All these shops sport a similar range of old (some faux) and new curios.
Cinnamon, *Stuba Hall, 1/658 Ridsdale Rd, Parade Ground, T0484-221 7124, www. cinnamonthestore.com*. Posh clothing, fabrics and interiors shop.
Idiom Books, *branches on VI/183 Synagogue Lane, Jew Town and Bastion Rd, T0484-221 7075*. Very good range on India, travel, fiction, religion, philosophy, etc.
Indian Industries, *Princess St, Fort Kochi, T0484-221 6448*. One of Fort Kochi's oldest antique dealers. Lovely family-run store with fixed prices and no-hassle browsing.

Ernakulam

There are several government emporia on MG Rd, Ernakulam, including **National Textiles** (another in Banerji Rd). Other shopping areas are in Broadway, Super Bazar, Anand Bazar, Prince St and New Rd.

What to do

Fort Kochi
Body and soul

Be Beautiful, *Princess St, T0484-221 5398. Open 0900-2030.* Good, cheap beauty salon with massage, hairdressers, pedicure and manicure in new premises.
Sanathana School of Yoga Studies, *XV/2188-D Beach Rd Junction, T0484-229 4155, www.sanathanayoga.com.* Daily classes 0730-0930 and 1630-1830, *pranayama* and *asanas* plus 28-day teacher training programmes in a pretty residence in downtown Fort Kochi.

Tour operators
Spice Land Holidays and Entertainments Private Limited, *Suite 2, Saniya Plaza, Rajaji Rd, T91484-237 8022, www.spicelandholidays.com.* Package and customized tours throughout Kerala and the rest of India.

Ernakulam
Tour operators

Hi Tours, *Jomer Arcade, South Junction, Chittoor Rd, T0484-237 7415, www.hi-tours.com.* Efficient and well-connected inbound travel agent, who can hook you up with homestays, authentic Ayurveda retreats and responsible tour operators throughout Kerala. Helpful and highly recommended.
KTDC, *Shanmugham Rd, Ernakulam, T0484-235 3234.* Full- and half-day backwater tours on *kettuvallams.*

Full-day tour 0830-1830 (includes lunch); half-day tour 0830-1300 and 1400-1830. Tours include visits to coir factory, spice garden, canoe ride and toddy tapping demonstration. Also daily half-day Kochi sightseeing boat cruises, 0900-1230 and 1400-1730, which cover Bolgatty Island, Chinese fishing nets, St Francis Church and Mattancherry Palace. Tour departs from Sealord Jetty.
Pioneer Personalized Holidays, *Pioneer House, 5th Cross, Willingdon Island, T0484-266 6148, www.pioneertravels.com.* Fleet of cars with tailor-made tour packages from a well-established and highly competent tour company. Efficient and knowledgeable, with unusual homestay and guesthouse options.
Sundale Vacations, *39/5955 Atlantis Junction, MG Rd, T0484-235 9127, www.sundale.com.* Surface and hotel arrangements in Kerala, specializes in homestays catering to 'foreign independent tourists', promoting insight into Kerala's customs. Programmes from US$467.
Tourist Desk, *Main Boat Jetty, T0484-237 1761, www.touristdesk.in.* One of the best budget tour operators. Daily backwater tours, 0800-1700, Rs 550, using both *kettuvalloms* and canoe. Tour includes visits to see coir making, spice garden, local village and lunch. Also 2- to 3-day tours to Wayanad and Kannur. Highly recommended.
Visit India, *North Janatha Rd, T0484-233 9045, www.visitindiatravel.com.* Half-day backwater tours in a dugout, punted and engineless, through very peaceful shady waterways passing unspoilt villages with toddy tappers, coir making, fishing, etc; led by an excellent guide. Highly recommended. Also offers trips in traditional *kettuvallams.*

Transport

Air

Kochi's airport is at Nedumbassery, 36 km northeast of the city, T0484-261 0012. Hotels charge Rs 900-1500 for airport pick-up, depending on type of car and what the market will support. Prepaid taxis charge around Rs 850 to Fort Kochi, a little less to downtown Ernakulam. A/c buses leave from outside the international terminal for Fort Kochi (Rs 80) via the new intercity bus stand at Vytilla Junction (Rs 60), 3 km west of Ernakulam centre.

Daily domestic flights to: **Bengaluru**, **Chennai**, **Mumbai**, **Delhi** via **Goa**, **Thiruvananthapuram**; and several flights per week to **Coimbatore**, **Hyderabad**, **Kozhikode** and **Tiruchirapalli**.

International flights to: **Abu Dhabi**, **Doha**, **Dubai**, **Kuala Lumpur**, **Kuwait**, **Muscat**, **Sharjah** (UAE) and **Singapore**.

Bus

Local Buses journey between Ernakulam, Willingdon and Fort Kochi frequently during the day. There are no local buses after 2100.

Long distance Buses run from the **KSRTC Bus Station**, Chavara Rd, T0484-237 2033, www.keralartc.com. There are frequent services to **Alappuzha**, every 20 mins (1½ hrs); **Kottayam**, every 30 mins (1½ hrs); **Kozhikode**, every 30 mins (5 hrs) and **Thiruvananthapuram**, every 30 mins (5 hrs). There are 7 departures daily to **Kumily** (6 hrs) or take a bus to Kottayam and change there. There is an 0630 departure to **Munnar** (4 hrs), and departures to **Kannur** at 1445 and 2345 (7 hrs). Interstate services include: 9 daily to **Bengaluru** (14 hrs) via **Kozhikode** (5 hrs) and **Mysore**

(10 hrs); **Kanniyakumari**, at 1430 (7½ hrs); and **Chennai** at 1400 (15 hrs) via **Coimbatore** (5 hrs).

Private operators run from **Kalloor** and **Ernakulam Southbus stands** including **Indira Travels**, DH Rd, T0484-236 0693; **SB Travels**, String Dew Building, Tripunithura, T0484-277 7949; and **Princy Tours**, opposite Sealord Hotel, T0484-237 3109, www.princytravels.com. Overnight coaches to **Bengaluru** (12 hrs) and **Mysore** (10 hrs). Departures every 30 mins to **Kottayam** (2 hrs) and **Munnar** (4 hrs). Also to **Chennai** and **Coimbatore**.

Ferry

Regular ferry services connect Ernakulam with Fort Kochi and are the fastest and easiest form of transport. Ferry tickets cost Rs 2.50. Most ferries take bikes and motorbikes. It's also possible to hire a motor boat for up to 20, from Sea Lord jetty in Ernakulam through the **KTDC** office.

Ernakulam Main Boat Jetty, Cannon Shed Rd. Ferries depart approximately every 30 mins to Fort Kochi 'Customs' jetty 0555-2130. There are also regular ferries to the Fort Kochi Mattancherry jetty (last departure to Mattancherry is 1845), and to Willingdon Island's 'Embarkation' Jetty from here. Ferries to Bolghatty depart from the High Court Jetty off Shanmugham Rd approximately every 20 mins Mon-Sat 0600-2100.

Fort Kochi Regular departures from Customs jetty 0620-2150. The last ferry leaves for Ernakulam from the Mattencherry jetty at 1930. From the northern Vypeen Jetty there are services every 30 mins to Vypeen Island between 0600-2130.

Willingdon Island There are 2 jetties: 'Embarkation' (north) and 'Terminus' (west). Ferries run every 30 mins to Ernakulam from 'Embarkation' from 0600-2110. From the 'Terminus' jetty there are infrequent services to Mattancherry on Fort Kochi.

Rickshaw

Auto-rickshaw drivers have a reasonably good reputation here. But, if you are likely to arrive late at night, insist on being taken directly to your hotel. A rickshaw between Fort Kochi and Ernakulam should cost around Rs 250. Fares within Fort Kochi or Ernakulam: Rs 30-60.

Taxi

Ernakulam Junction to Fort Kochi, Rs 400. To airport, Rs 700.

Train

Ernakulam/Kochi is on the broad gauge line joining Thiruvananthapuram to Mangalore, Bengaluru and Chennai. Most trains from major cities stop at **Ernakulam Junction** (the main station, booking code: ERS) although a few stop at Ernakulam Town (ERN), T0484-239 0920. Enquiries: Ernakulam Junction, T131 or T0484-237 5131.

Trains to: **Bengaluru**: 3 daily, 11 hrs, via Thrissur (1 hr), Palakkad (2½-4 hrs) and Coimbatore (5 hrs); **Chennai**: 7-10 a day (12 hrs); **Mangalore**: 7-10 a day (10 hrs) via **Thrissur**, **Kozhikode** (4 hrs) and **Kannur** (5-6 hrs); **Thiruvananthapuram**, more than 20 a day, all via **Kollam** and **Varkala**; and **Tiruchirappali**, 1 daily (9 hrs), continues to **Thanjavur** (10 hrs).

Munnar &
Idukki's high ranges

Inland from the plains around Kottayam and Kochi lie the foothills of the Western Ghats, swathed in tropical evergreen forests and an ever-creeping tide of monoculture rubber plantations. As you climb higher these give way to pepper and cardamom, until finally you reach the rolling tea plantations and rarefied air of landlocked Idukki District. To the south sits Thekkady and the unmissable Periyar National Park, home to tiger, wild elephant, and an innovative project that is steadily turning yesterday's poachers into tomorrow's tour guides.

Munnar, meanwhile, five hours uphill from Kochi, is *chai* central: a surreal rippling mosaic of yellow-green tea bushes and red dust roads stretching from valley deep to mountain high, with dark granite peaks pointing like fingers toward the bald grassy dome of South India's highest mountain, Anaimudi. At 1600 m, Munnar is much higher than Thekkady and gets genuinely cold, a fact that made it a favourite summer bolthole for the Raj. Wildlife tourists flock to the nearby Eravikulam National Park for a glimpse of the endangered but semi-tame Nilgiri thar, a variety of ibex, while further to the north are the forests and deeply etched ravines of magnificent, rarely visited Chinnar Wildlife Sanctuary.

Essential Munnar and Idukki's high ranges

Finding your feet

The nearest transport hub for Munnar is Kochi-Ernakulam; Thekkady (Periyar Reserve/Kumily town) is best accessed from Kottayam. There are no train links to the high ranges; buses take a minimum of four hours to climb the hills to both hill stations, and roads linking the two take the same length of time. For details, see Transport, page 101.

Fact...

The first rubber plantation was cultivated in 1902. India is now among the top three rubber producers worldwide, and most of that comes from Kerala. Crops in Kerala are determined by height: tea grows above 1500 m, cardamom, coffee and other spices between 1500 m and 600 m, coconut and rubber below 600 m.

The Midlands (Kottayam to Thekkady)

from the plains to the hills, with excellent views over the ghats

An interesting drive to the hills, this route follows the ghat road, which has superb views down the east side of the ghats onto the Tamil Nadu plains. You may meet herds of Zebu cattle, buffalo and donkeys being driven from Tamil Nadu to market in Kerala. Above 1000 m the air freshens and it can be cold. Be prepared for a rapid change in temperature.

Pala

Lying off the Kottayam–Thekkady road, Pala is a town famous for its learned citizens – graduates of the European-style Gothic university, which was built, along with the Gothic church, by one of its affluent sons. Nehru visited in the 1950s and said that Pala was full of "people of vision". The town was the most literate place in India long before Kerala achieved 100% literacy, and Meenachil Taluka has the highest proportion of educated women in the country. It is also famous for its tamarind and pepper as well as the rubber estates belonging to the Dominic family, who serve hot Syrian-Catholic lunches in their 100-year-old plantation bungalow and 50-year-old estate mansion. Plantation tours to watch latex collection and packing can be arranged through **CGH Earth**, see page 64.

Erattupetta and Vagamon

Further east lies **Erattupetta**, whose grey St George's Church holds naïve wood-painted doves and disembodied cherubims, and which hosts the **High Range Festival** every April. Carry on for **Vagamon**, a village set on a chain of three hills: Thangal, Murugal and Kurisumala. A dairy farm here is managed by Kurisumala monks.

Peermade

Some 25 km south from Vagamon is Peermade, named after Peer Mohammed, a Sufi saint and crony of the royal family of Travancore. It is surrounded by tea,

A modern mass pilgrimage

Sabarimala pilgrims are readily visible in many parts of South India as they wear black *dhotis* as a symbol of the penance they must undergo for 41 days before they make the pilgrimage. In addition to the black dress, pilgrims must take two baths daily and only eat food at home during this period. The pilgrimage, which begins at Deepavali, is only for males and prepubescent and post-menstrual females, to avoid the defilement believed to be associated with menstruation.

"The pilgrimage in January is deliberately hard", writes Vaidyanathan, because "the pilgrimage to the shrine symbolizes the struggle of the individual soul in its onward journey to the abode of bliss and beatitude. The path of the spiritual aspirant is always long, arduous and hazardous. And so is the pilgrimage to Sabarimala, what with the observance of severe austerities and trekking up forested mountains, risking attacks from wild animals".

rubber and cardamom plantations, including **Abraham's Spice Garden**, where a member of the family gives excellent spice tours. Buses between Kottayam and Kumily can drop you here.

Sabarimala

Hidden away in the hills to the south is Sabarimala, the focus of what some say is the world's biggest annual pilgrimage: 55 million Hindu pilgrims a year, almost all men, trek through the forest to the shrine, which is where the god Ayyappan is believed to have meditated after slaying a demoness. Aiyappan is a particularly favoured deity in Kerala and there are growing numbers of devotees. For details of the pilgrimage, see box, above. The shrine is only open on specific occasions: **Mandalam**, mid-November to the end of December; **Makaravilakku**, mid-January; **Vishu**, mid-April; **Prathistha** one day in May-June; and during the Onam festival in August-September.

Listings The Midlands (Kottayam to Thekkady)

Where to stay

$$$$ **Kottukapally Nazarani Tharavad**
Palai, T(0)9846-212438,
www.nazaranitharavad.com.
An opportunity to stay with the Kottukapally family (Kerala political royalty). There are grand Byzantine icons, Persian carpets and Travancore brass lamps. The roomy 250-year-old Kerala/

Dutch/Spanish-style house of teak, rosewood and Basel tiles has 3 roomy doubles. Book in advance.

$$$$ **Serenity Kanam**
At Kanam Estate, 25 km east of Kottayam off Kumily Rd, T0481-245 6353, www.malabarhouse.com.
This wonderful villa hotel has just 6 huge rooms, decorated with quality art and sculpture, set in a gently restored

1920s bungalow surrounded by rubber plantations and spice gardens. There's a big pool, spa and excellent food, and you can spend a morning exploring the quiet lanes from the back of Lakshmi, the estate elephant. Far from any sights, but it's worth building in an extra night or 2 just to stay here.

$$$ The Pimenta
Haritha Farms, The Pimenta, Kadalikad Post, T0485-226 02160, www.thepimenta.in.
An eco-tourism concern in a pepper-growing region. Guest numbers are limited to minimize impact on the village. 4 newly built simple cottages close to the family farmhouse. The family are advocates of the return to traditional methods of agriculture, Haritha grows bio-organic spices, medicinal herbs and tropical fruit and re-plants crops lost to monoculture tea and rubber plantations. All meals included.

$$$ Vanilla County
Mavady Estate, Teekoy, Vagamon, T(0)9744-183835, www.vanillacounty.in.
At the source of the Meenachil River. A charming, family-friendly place with 3 rooms within 60-year-old estate house that you share with your hosts. Coffee is from the plantation around you and you can swim in nearby natural ponds. Internet access. Price includes all meals.

Covering 930 sq km of montane forest and grassland and centred on an attractive lake, the Periyar National Park, 115 km east of Kottayam, may not throw up many tiger sightings nowadays but still attracts more than 300,000 visitors a year for its beautiful setting and unique range of soft adventure activities. Elephants, *gaur* and wild boar, though by no means guaranteed, are regularly spotted from the lake cruise boats, while sloth bear, porcupine and Malabar giant squirrel also haunt the woods. Wild boar forage along the lakeside, butterflies as big as bats bounce beneath the canopies of prehistoric jack trees, and you'll hear the thud-thwack-holler as unruly gangs of Nilgiri langur swoop through the high branches of giant figs.

The sanctuary was established by the old Travancore State government in 1934 and brought under the umbrella of Project Tiger in 1973, but Periyar's finest hour came in 1998 when the Kerala Forest Department, in partnership with the World Bank and the Thekkady Wildlife Society (a local NGO), set up a project to deploy a band of reformed cinnamon poachers from the surrounding villages as tour leaders and forest rangers in remote parts of the park. The camo-clad members of the **Ex-Vayana Bark Collectors Eco Development Committee** now earn a steady income from tourism, not to mention new-found respect within their communities, and

Essential Periyar National Park

Finding your feet

With the exception of a couple of government-run hotels down by the lakeside, everything that happens in Periyar happens in the busy little tourist trap of Kumily. The bus stand is at the north end of the main street, a 10-minute walk from most hotels. Buses run down to the lake jetty, or you can hire a bike (a tough ride back up the hill without gears), take an auto-rickshaw, share a jeep, or take the pleasant walk through the woods. For details, see Transport, page 94.

When to go

The best time to visit is December to April, when dry weather brings animals closer to the lake. Dawn and dusk are best for wildlife, so stay overnight (winter nights can get quite cold). Avoid weekends and holidays, and especially the Makaravilakku festival in mid-January, which brings pilgrims by their millions to the Sabarimala shrine (see box, page 87).

Tip...

Overnight treks into the park's hinterland offer an unmatched opportunity to see big animals up close and on foot, but even on a day visit Periyar can show you some impressive nature.

Entry fees

Entry to the park costs Rs 300 per day, Rs 105 for children; Indians pay Rs 25/Rs 5.

their hard-won knowledge of the terrain and sharp instincts for animal behaviour makes them skilled, if not exactly chatty, forest guides. Trekking with them for a day represents your best chance of getting up close with elephants.

The centre of activities in the park is the boat jetty at Thekkady on pretty **Lake Periyar**, 3 km down a beautiful forest road from the tourist village of **Kumily**, which was created in 1895 by a dam that inundated 55 sq km of rich forest. A 180-m-long tunnel now leads the water eastward into the Suruli and Vaigai rivers, irrigating extensive areas of Ramanathapuram and Madurai districts in Tamil Nadu.

Exploring the park

The standard way to see Periyar is to take a trip across the lake on a **motor launch** ⓘ *depart 0730, 0930, 1115, 1345 and 1530, Rs 150; tickets on sale 90 mins before departure, no advance reservation required.* You can get good wildlife sightings on the first trip of the morning – elephants, gaur, wild boar, sambar and barking deer are regularly spotted browsing on the banks, and packs of dhole (wild dog) very occasionally seen. However, noisy boats (and their occupants) and the heat soon drive animals away from the shore. Jeeps begin queueing at the park entrance gate from 0500 to get on the first launch of the morning, and there's a mad sprint to the ticket office once you reach the lake's edge.

At the Eco Tourism Office in Kumily you can book a 2½-hour **forest trek** ⓘ *maximum 6 people, depart 0700, 0730, 1000, 1030, 1400, 1430, Rs 200 per person (minimum Rs. 800 per trek), no advance reservations so get to office early to queue; carry water and beware of leeches.* There are good chances of seeing Malabar giant squirrel and Nilgiri langur, but much depends on your guide and not everybody

Periyar National Park

Where to stay 🛏	Green View **1**	Spice Village **5**
Cardomom County **6**	Lake Palace **9**	Treetop **8**
Carmelia Haven **11**	Mickey Farm House **13**	
Chrissie's **16**	Paradisa Plantation	**Restaurants 🍴**
Claus Garden **2**	Resort **10**	Ebony's Cafe **1**
Coffee Inn & Restaurant **3**	Periyar House **7**	French Restaurant **2**
Deer Villa **15**	Rose Garden Homestay **14**	

comes face to face with a herd of elephants; some return very disappointed. Guides may also offer to arrange unofficial private walking tours in the park periphery in the afternoon (not the best time for spotting wildlife); try to assess the guide before signing up.

A more rewarding option is to sign up for one of the longer adventures into the park offered by the **Ex-Vayana Bark Collectors Eco Development Committee**. If you only have a day to spend in the park, spend it on the **bamboo rafting trip** ⓘ *minimum 2 and maximum 10 people Rs 1500 per person (minimum Rs 3000 per trip)*, a full-day odyssey on land and water, trekking through a mosaic of grasslands, dense forest and rocky lakeshore, and navigating a long stretch of the lake on rickety rafts. Bird sightings are fabulous, with great hornbill a real possibility, and the ex-poacher guides have been known to change the route to pursue – in a strictly non-violent sense – herds of elephant. A rifleman accompanies every group to ward off the threat of a charge.

If you've got longer, the **Tiger Trail** covers much the same ground but offers a chance to trek deeper into the forest, camping out for one or two nights (Rs 4000/6000 per person, maximum of six guests). Other activities include the **Jungle Patrol** (a three-hour night trek, where you might spotlight porcupine and nightjars); the full-day **Border Hiking Trail** to a peak overlooking the Kambam Valley; and **bullock cart rides** to a traditional farming village.

Around Thekkady

There are a number of attractions within easy reach of Thekkady. These include the traditional Keralite-style **Mangaladevi Temple**, set amongst dense woodland on the peak of a 1337 m hill, 15 km northeast of Thekkady. Permission to visit the area must be obtained from the Wildlife Warden in Thekkady, though the temple itself is only open during the **Chithra Pounami** holiday. Other picturesque spots around Thekkady include **Pandikuzhi** (5 km) and **Chellarkovil** (15 km).

Listings Periyar National Park (Thekkady) *map p90*

Tourist information

District Tourism Office
Kumily, T0486-922 2620.
Runs plantation tours to Abraham's Spice Garden (4 km) and Vandiperiyar (18 km).

Eco Tourism Office
Ambady Junction, Kumily, T0486-922 4571, www.periyartigerreserve.org.
Has information and books tickets for all treks and tours in the Periyar National Park.

Where to stay

Check www.thekkady.com for information.

$$$$ Lake Palace
Lake Periyar, T0486-922 3887, www.lakepalacethekkady.com.
6 rooms in an interesting building inside the reserve. Idyllic island setting with superb views and wildlife spotting. Access by free ferry (20 mins) from jetty (last trip 1600). Relaxed and informal. Rates include all meals.

$$$$ Paradisa Plantation Retreat
Murinjapuzha, Kottayam–Kumily Rd,
T0469-270 1311, www.paradisaretreat.com.
10 traditionally built new cottages
with beautiful antique granite pillars
and room furnishings, on an organic
plantation estate with stunning valley
views and a pool. Yoga recommended
but booking essential.

$$$$ Spice Village (CGH Earth)
Thekkady–Kumily Rd, T0486-922 4514,
www.cghearth.com. Discounts Apr-Sep.
Cottages with elephant grass thatch
(cool and dark with wide eaves), spice
garden, badminton, tennis, good pool,
yoga centre. Excellent restaurant, lunch
and dinner buffets (Rs 500), chilled beer.
Good cookery demonstrations, great
Ayurvedic massage and forest walks to
see smaller wildlife. Luxurious, quiet,
restful, friendly, with superb service.

$$$$-$$$ Cardamom County
Thekkady Rd, T0486-922 4501,
www.raxacollective.com.
Spacious, comfortable cottages, good
restaurant, nice pool, friendly (request
off-season discount). Recommended.

$$$ Hotel Treetop
Thekkady Rd, T0486-922 3286,
www.hoteltreetop.com.
Clean and efficient resort of gabled
cottages with all mod cons and private
balconies, just on the fringes of the
Periyar National Park. Family bungalow
has a kitchen and living area. Library,
restaurant, Ayurveda massages available.

$$$-$$ Carmelia Haven
Vandanmedu (20 km north on
Puliyanmala Rd), T0486-827 0272,
www.carmeliahaven.com.
On a tea, spice and coconut plantation,
exclusive and private, with a treehouse

6 m above ground, a cave house 3 m
below, and a few discreetly spaced
cottages in a local style using lots of
thatch. An excellent open-air restaurant
serves delicious Malabari food. Tours
of tea factory, cardamom plantations,
treks and boating. Tea and cardamom
for sale.

$$ Periyar House (KTDC)
5 mins' walk from the lake,
T04869-222026, www.periyar
housethekkady.com.
Pleasant, clean and comfortable rooms.
Buffet meals and strong Goan beer
available. Good service.

$$-$ Chrissie's
Thekkady Bypass Rd, T0486-922 4155,
www.chrissies.in.
Rs 1800-2800 (including taxes). Modern
minimalist rooms all with balcony. Lush,
peaceful garden with shady seating
areas to relax in. Restaurant, yoga studio.

$$-$ Claus Garden
Rosapukandam, 10 mins' uphill
from bus stand behind post office,
3rd turning on the right, T0486-
922 2320, www.homestay.in.
Spacious rooms in a peaceful house
surrounded by jungle. Funky communal
area, book exchange, friendly chilled-
out vibe.

$$-$ Coffee Inn
Thekkady Rd, 5 mins' walk from entrance
gate, T0486-922 2763,
www.coffeeinnthekkady.com.
Wide variety of rooms, cheaper huts in
quiet garden annex 100 m down the
road. Popular budget traveller hang-out.
Restaurant, book exchange, friendly. No
reservations – rooms are allocated on a
first come first served basis.

$ Deer Villa
Thekkady Bypass Rd, T0486-922 3568,
www.deervilla.com.
Friendly family home boasting clean,
airy rooms with balcony, fan and hot
water. Breakfast included. Internet
café downstairs.

$ Green View
Hotel Ambadi Junction, Thekkady
Bypass Rd, T0486-922 4617,
www.sureshgreenview.com.
Suresh and Sulekha run a welcoming
'home away from home' in a rambling
house surrounded by mango trees.
Hammocks are slung out in the garden.
All 16 spotlessly clean rooms have large
bathrooms (towels, loo roll and soap
provided). Standard and deluxe rooms
have cable TV and balcony. Suresh is an
ex-tour guide and can provide maps for
mountain treks and walks in the area.
Meals available on request, cookery
classes, breakfast included. Friendly
and helpful.

$ Mickey Farm House
Thekkady Bypass Rd, T0486-922 3196,
www.mickeyhomestay.com.
Pleasant airy rooms in pretty garden,
all with balcony. Cheaper rooms with
outside bath. Mickey runs 4- to 7-day
treks to Kottayam/Alappuzha (advance
notice required). Friendly family,
excellent value. Recommended.

$ Rose Garden Homestay
Hotel Ambadi Junction, Thekkady
Bypass Rd, T0486-922 3146,
www.rosegardenhomestay.com.
Sathi has 6 simply furnished rooms,
all with TV, in the back garden of her
flowered house. Lots of hanging wicker
chairs on porches. Lovely family provides
traditional Keralite breakfasts and
suppers. Discounts for long stays.

Restaurants

$$$ Spice Village
See Where to stay.
International, excellent food and service,
rustic decor, fresh garden vegetables
and chef's cooking show nightly.

$$ Coffee Inn
See Where to stay. Open 0700-2200.
International dishes served at tables
outside under the palms, bonfire in
the evening, relaxed and peaceful.
Friendly but very slow service.

$ Ebony's Café
Thekkady Bypass Rd.
Rooftop restaurant with huge range
of Indian and international dishes.

$ Edassery's Farm Yard
NH 49 Chattupara Adimali Idukki,
T04864-224210. Open 0600-2200.
Makes a good break on the Kottayam–
Kumily road with tasty soups and meals,
dosa and vegetable stews.

$ French Restaurant
Thekkady Rd, T(0)9961-213107.
Good bread, muesli, snacks and coffee.

$ Our Place
Next to Jungle View Homestay,
Rosappukandam.
Run by a British/Indian couple, this
cosy café serves comfort food from
back home alongside excellent Indian
vegetarian options.

Entertainment

Kadathanadan Kalari Centre, *Thekkady*
Rd, Kumily, T(0)9961-740868, www.
thekkadytourism.in. 1-hr demonstration
of Kerala's traditional martial art,
Kalarippayattu. Show time 1800, Rs 200,
video charge Rs 250. Also Kathakali
shows 1700-1800 and 1900-2000

Mudra Daily Kathakali Centre,
Thekkady Rd, Kumily, T0486-922 2303,
www.mudraculturalcentre.com. Classical
dance theatre show by performers
from Kalamandalam school of dance.
Kathakali 1700, 1900; Kalari 1800, 1915;
Rs 200, video charge Rs 200.

What to do

Tours
Eco Tourism Information Centre,
Hotel Ambadi Junction, Thekkady Bypass
Rd, Kumily, T0486-922 2620, www.
periyartigerreserve.org. Organizes a full
range of tours within the park: bamboo
rafting, tiger trails with 1 or 2 nights'
camping, evening jungle patrols, border
hiking and treks to tribal settlements.

Transport

Beware of 3-wheelers and guides at
the bus station, who are working on
commission from guesthouses. Nearly all
hotels in Kumily are within a 10-min walk
of the bus station.

Bus Local: Minibuses hourly from
Kumily go down to **Aranya Nivas** on the
lakeside, Rs 2. At Kumily jeep drivers will
tell you there is no bus to Thekkady and
charge Rs 50 for the trip; autos charge
Rs 25 plus.

   Long distance: From Kumily:
frequent services to **Kottayam**, every
20 mins from 0600 (4½ hrs). Regular buses
to **Kochi/Ernakulam**, 6 per day, 1st at
0600 (6½ hrs); **Alappuzha**, 6 per day,
1st at 0600 (6 hrs); **Thiruvanantha-**
puram, 3 per day, 1st at 0830 (8 hrs);
Munnar, 5 per day, 1st at 0600 (4½ hrs).
Daily bus to **Kodaikkanal** (cancelled
occasionally), 0630 (5½ hrs), or go to
Vathalakundu and change. Buses also
go from Thekkady itself (behind Aranya
Nivas): frequent departures to **Madurai**,
every 20 mins, from 0600 (4 hrs).

A major centre of Kerala's tea industry, Munnar (altitude 1520 m) sits in the lee of Anaimudi, South India's highest peak at 2695 m, and is the nearest Kerala comes to a genuine hill station. The landscape is European Alpine, minus the snow, plus tea bushes – inestimable millions of them. The town is surrounded by about 30 tea estates, among them the highest in the world at Kolukkumalai, yet despite the increasingly commercial use of the hills you can still find forests that are rich in wildlife, including the endangered Nilgiri tahr. The workers on the tea estates are mostly Tamilians who moved here eight or nine generations ago.

The surrounding hills are also home to the rare Neelakurunji orchid (*Strobilanthes*), which covers the hills in colour for a month once every 12 years (next due 2018). During the monsoon, cotton wool swabs of cloud shift and eddy across hillsides, sodden as a sponge with fresh rains, and springs burst their banks and surge across the pathways where villagers, dark-skinned tribals in ski jackets and woollen noddy hats, swing past on Enfields on their way home from a day on the tea plantations.

The road from Kochi

The route from Kochi to Munnar is one of South India's most attractive ghat roads. The one sight of note is the is the 25-sq-km **Salim Ali Bird Sanctuary** ⓘ *Thattekad, 70 km east of Kochi on a side road heading north out of Kothamangalam; contact Assistant Wildlife Warden, Thattekad, T0485-258 8302.* A tropical evergreen and semi-evergreen forest with teak and rosewood plantations, the sanctuary is surrounded by the Periyar River, which remains shallow most of the year. It attracts water birds and the indigenous Malabar grey hornbill, rose and blue-winged parakeet, egret, heron and mynah, while rarer birds like the Ceylon frog-mouth and rose-billed rollers are also sometimes seen here.

Sights

Tata Tea Museum ⓘ *Nullatanni Estate, T04865-230561, www.keralatourism.org, open 0900-1600, Rs 50, closed Mon.* The museum has a heap of artefacts, curios and photographs to help conjure something of the lives of the men who opened up the High Ranges to tea. The crop has grown here for over a century so relics include a rudimentary tea roller from 1905 and a wheel from the Kundale Valley Light Railway that used to transport men and materials between Munnar and Top Station. The museum has descriptions of the

Essential Munnar

Finding your feet

The easiest access is by bus or taxi from Kochi. There are also daily buses to Kumily and major towns in Kerala and Tamil Nadu. The town is small and pleasant for exploring on foot, although there are autos. It is worth hiring a bike or a jeep for trips out of town. See Transport, page 101.

Munnar

Where to stay
Arafa Tourist Home 1
East End 3
Isaac's Residency 4
John's Cottage 5
Nature Zone 6
Olive Brook 7
Tall Trees 10
Tea County 11
Theresian Cottages 12
Windermere Estate 13
Zeena Cottages 14

Restaurants
Saravana Bhavan 1
Silver Spoon 2

Bars & clubs
High Range Club 3
KDH Club 4

fully automated technology of today from the tea factory at Madupatty. The museum can also arrange a visit to this factory, watching tea pickers at work and seeing how the tea is processed.

Christ Church In the centre of Old Munnar, set on a hill immediately above the road in the centre of town, Christ Church was built to serve tea estate managers and workers of the High Ranges. The last English-language service was held in 1981; it is now shared between protestant Tamil and Malayalam worshippers. The exterior is un-preposessing: rather squat and now blackened by weathering, but inside it is a charming small church and still contains its original 14 rows of wooden pews. Ask to see the diminutive record of births and deaths of the town's founders, the British planters.

Immediately behind the church a zigzag path up the hill leads to the small pioneer **cemetery** that was established long before the church itself as the chosen burial ground of Mrs Eleanor Knight, General Manager Knight's 24-year-old bride who caught cholera after arriving in the High Range in 1894.

Mount Carmel Roman Catholic Church The first Catholic church in the High Ranges, Mount Carmel is in Old Munnar on the road up to the Tata General Hospital. The first chapel on the site was founded in 1898 by Friar Alphonse who arrived in Munnar from Spain in 1854. The present church was built by the then Bishop of Vijayapuram in 1938.

High Range Club ⓘ *T04865-230253, www.highrangeclubmunnar.com.* This private members' club is more relaxed than the famously 'Snooty' Ooty Club. A tradition allowed members to hang their hats on the wall of the bar after 30 years of belonging to the club – the last was hung in 1989 to make 51 hats in all. Saturday is strictly jacket and tie only and backpackers will need to scrub up well to get in any day of the week. "We like scholars and researchers, professionals and club people", says the club secretary, "they know how to move in a club". It's a wonderful place with teak floors, squash courts, library and fascinating planters to chat to if you're interested in the planters' social history.

Around Munnar

There are some excellent **cycle rides** around Munnar, not all of them steep. One ride goes up a gentle slope through a beautiful valley 8 km to the **Letchmi Estate**. There is a *chai* stall at the estate and the road continues to the head of the valley for views down to the forest. A second ride (or walk) leaves Munnar by the south road for 3 km, turning left at the Head Works Dam, then takes a right turn past Copper Castle, then left to a tea stall, viewpoint, tea and cardamom plantations, again with superb views. Continue to the next tea pickers' village for a tea stall. A shorter option for this route is to cross the dam and turn left, taking the quiet road north to the **High Range Club** and Munnar.

Mattupetty Lake ⓘ *13 km from Munnar, T04865-230389, visits 0900-1100, 1400-1530, Rs 5.* At an altitude of 1700 m, Mattupetty Lake is flanked by steep hills and woods. It was created by the small hydroelectricity dam. To its south is the Kerala Livestock Development Board's research and cattle breeding centre, formerly the Indo-Swiss dairy project. In a beautiful semi-Alpine setting surrounded for much of the year by lush green fields, the centre offers interesting insights into the practical realities and achievements of cattle breeding in India today.

Top Station Some 34 km from Munnar on the Tamil Nadu border, at an altitude of 2100 m, Top Station has some of the highest tea estates in India. It is an idyllic spot, with superb views over the Tamil Nadu plains and the edge of the Western Ghats. Stalls serve tea and soft drinks. Top Station took its name from a ropeway that connected it via Middle Station to Lower Station at the valley bottom.

The small town of **Bodinayakkanur**, which can be reached on the Devikulam road, lies in the valley. Buses leave from the shelter north of Munnar post office at 0715, 0915 and 1115 bound for Kovilor, passing Mattupetty Lake and Kundala Dam. Get off at Top Station, return bus after about one hour.

Kolukkumalai Across the valley from Top Station, and around 40 km east of Munnar, the small plantation of Kolukkumalai officially claims to pick the highest tea leaves in the world. The drive to the ridgetop at 2175 m takes two hours (the last section on a plantation road so bad it might be quicker to get out and walk) but the effort is repaid by astonishing views across misty valleys and distant peaks. It's worth being here for sunrise; set off by 0400 and wrap up warm for the journey. A path through the tea bushes leads down to the 1930s factory, where you can sample the local product and watch the antique processing equipment in action. As the plantation is privately owned you need to join a tour to get in; **Kestrel Adventures** (see What to do, page 100) is the main operator.

Eravikulam/Rajamalai National Park ① *21 km northeast of Munnar, www. eravikulam.org, closed Feb-Mar and during the monsoons, Rs 370.* The park was set up in 1978 to preserve the endangered Nilgiri tahr (*Nilgiri ibex*). The conservation programme has resulted in the park now supporting the largest population of the species in the world, of nearly 2000. The sure-footed wild goats live in herds on the steep black rocky slopes of the Anaimudi Mountains. They are brownish, have short, flat horns with the male carrying a thick mane, and can be easily seen around the park entrance. There are also elephants, sambars, gaurs, macaques and the occasional leopard and tiger. The scenery is magnificent, though the walks into the forest are steep and strenuous. There is an easier paved path from the park entrance following the road immediately below the bare granite outcrop of the Naikundi Hill to the Rajamalai Gap. The Forest Department issues a limited number of permits to trek through the park on the **Goldsbury Track**.

Chinnar Wildlife Sanctuary ① *Contact the Forest Information Office in Munnar, T04865-231587.* Adjoining Eravikulam to the north, and spreading down the eastern slope of the ghats into Tamil Nadu, Chinar Wildlife Sanctuary is rarely visited but offers near-guaranteed sightings of elephant and bison. Accommodation is in the form of treehouses and log huts.

Listings Munnar *map p96*

Tourist information

DTPC
Old Munnar Bazar, Munnar, T0486-231516, www.dtpcidukki.com.
The DTPC runs tours of plantations and rents cycles. Try also the free **Tourist Information Service** in the Main Bazar opposite the bus stop, run by Joseph Iype, a veritable mine of information. For trekking information, Senthil Kumar of local eco-guiding outfit **Kestrel Adventures** (see page 100) is hard to beat.

Where to stay

Hotel prices throughout Munnar are high for what you get, particularly in the summer high season. Cheaper places can be found around the bazar and bus stand, where touts will greet you brandishing the cards of 25-room concrete block 'cottages'.

The road from Kochi

$$$$-$$$ Plantation Homestay
Mundackal Estate, Pindimana, Kothamangalam Junction, T0485-257 0717.
4 rooms in a homestay that lies deep inside a rubber, pepper and coconut

plantation. Daisy is a mean cook and offers lessons (US$20), while George arranges boat trips to the bird sanctuary.

$$$ Periyar River Lodge
Anakkayam, Kothamanagalam, T(0)9526-100118, www.periyarriverlodge.com.
2-bedroom cottage in a rubber plantation on the banks of Periyar River right next to Thattekad Bird Sanctuary. Bamboo rafting, fishing, forest treks, jeep safaris to 30-m-high waterfalls for swimming, boat and bike tours. Lounge, en suite, river views. Keralite food.

Munnar

$$$$-$$$ Nature Zone
Pullipara, 5 km up dirt track off Letchmi Rd, west of TN Bus Stand, T(0)9745-433330.
Arriving here is like stepping into Jurassic Park – you have to get out of the car and unhook the elephant-repelling electric fence. A leading outward-bound training centre with stunning valley views, the drawcards here are the jungly remoteness and the 2 rustic-chic treehouses, with branches growing right through the room. The safari tents down at ground level are okay, but get pretty musty, and maintenance can leave a bit to be desired. On-site canteen serves good food.

$$$$-$$$ Tall Trees
Bison Valley Rd, 3 km south of Munnar, T(0)9447-111726, www.ttr.in.
A drastic price hike means the rather musty cottages here offer dubious value, but the location, beneath a canopy of ancient rainforest, is undeniably magic.

$$$$-$$$ Windermere Estate
Pothamedu, T04865-230512, www.windermeremunnar.com.
Standalone cottages and an alpine farmhouse with 5 rooms and an elegant

and utterly comfortable planters' bungalow with 3 rooms. The whole complex is set around an enormous granite boulder, that offers sweeping views of cloud-draped mountains, and there's a fantastically light and airy reading room done out with rustic timber furniture and vaulted ceilings. Pricey but recommended.

$$$ Tea County (KTDC)
1 km north of Munnar, T04865-230460, www.teacountymunnar.com.
67 immaculately kept rooms set in 3 ha of neat garden, good facilities, beautiful views, great walking, own transport essential.

$$$-$$ East End
Temple Rd, Munnar, T04865-230451, www.eastend.in.
18 pleasant rooms and some cottages (solar heated water), good but pricey restaurant, attractively designed, quiet garden location.

$$$-$$ Olive Brook
Bison Valley Rd, Pothamedu, 3 km south of Munnar, T04865-230588, www.olivebrookmunnar.com.
9 well-appointed but slowly declining double rooms in beautiful lush location on a cardamom farm, excellent alfresco barbecues on request. Price includes meals, trekking and cookery classes.

$$ Isaac's Residency
Top Station Rd, Munnar, T04865-230501.
Excellent quality, 32 lovely rooms with contemporary furnishings, Executive rooms with great views, 2 restaurants, bar. Recommended.

$$ John's Cottage
MSA Rd, near Munnar Supply Association, T(0)9447-331831, www. johnscottagehomestaymunnar.com.

Small bungalow home in a well-tended lawn running down to the river, with 8 clean rooms. Indian/Chinese food or use of kitchen.

$$-$ Zina Cottages
Near Hill View Hotel in Tata tea plantation, T04865-230349, www.zinacottagesmunnar.com.
Basic and slightly gloomy rooms in a colonial house, but the owners are friendly and the plantation views spectacular. Ask at the **Tourist Information Service** in the bazar (see page 98).

$ Arafa Tourist Home
Upper Bazar, Munnar, T04865-230788.
Riverside lodge with 14 non-a/c rooms with TV and phone. Handy for late-night bus arrivals. Noise travels, but the rooms are clean and good value.

$ Theresian Cottages
North of Munnar before Tea County, T0773-6434405.
3 rooms open off the shared living room of this sweet little 1930s house, and though they're fairly small and dark, each comes with a fireplace, chaise-longue and clean bathroom.

Restaurants

$$ The Greens
East End (see Where to stay).
Pleasant, glassed-in veranda serving good food, or go for the cheap simple meals in the eatery below.

$ Saravana Bhavan
MG Rd.
Clean, cheap and friendly place serving great *dosas* and huge Kerala-style *thalis* on banana leaves.

Bars and clubs

High Range Club
T04865-230253, www.highrangeclubmunnar.com.
Charming colonial-style planters' club, members only (or with reciprocal arrangements), visit by asking a planter to introduce you.

KDH Club
On side road opposite DTPC office.
For Tata staff, old-world, visit with permission, excellent pool table.

Shopping

Good for tea, cardamom and pepper.

Munnar Supply Assoc (MSA), *next to tourist information.* Established in 1900, it's a bit of the old world, where you can get everything. Tailors in the bazar can copy your garments in 24 hrs. The newer Main Bazar is to the north.
Uravu, *near Ambady Junction, Idukki, T(0)9387-469369, www.uravu.org.* Fair trade outfit supporting local producers of agrihorticultural products, bamboo products, processed foods, handicrafts, forest honey, spices tea and coffee.

What to do

DTPC, *see Tourist information, page 98.* Runs tours to Tea Valley (0900-1800, Rs 400) and Sandal Valley and Wildlife (1000-1800, Rs 400).
Kestrel Adventures, *PB No 44, Top Station Rd, T(0)9447-031040, www.kestreladventures.com.* Senthil Kumar leads a team of 9 specialist guides, some expert in birds, others in tea growing and history. Highly recommended for camping and trekking, wildlife spotting in Chinnar Wildlife Sanctuary, and the only company in town that can get you

into Kolukkumalai for sunrise. Also offers rock climbing, mountain bike tours/hire and jeep safaris.

Transport

Bike hire From the tourist information office, Rs 50 per day. **Kestrel Adventures** (see What to do) has 18-speed mountain bikes.

Bus State buses start and terminate at 2 separate stands south of town, but also call at the **Town Bus Stand** near the market. Enquiries, T04865-230201. Frequent services to **Mattupetty** (30 mins), **Devikulam** (30 mins), **Adimali** (1 hr) and **Top Station** (1 hr). Daily to **Coimbatore** (6 hrs); **Ernakulam/Kochi** (4½ hrs); **Kodaikkanal** 0700 via **Udumalpettai**, change for Palani and Kodai. If the Palani–Kodai Rd is closed a further bus goes to Vatalakundu and then Kodai; **Kottayam** (5 hrs); **Madurai** via **Theni** (5 hrs); **Thekkady** (4½ hrs), leaves from stop next to the post office; **Thiruvananthapuram** (9 hrs), **Thrissur** via **Perumbavoor** (5 hrs).

Jeeps/taxis Shared jeeps and minibus taxis for **Eravikulam** and **Mattupetty Lake** wait around the post office.

Thrissur, Palakkad
& the River Nila

The blue thread of the River Nila, Kerala's equivalent of the Ganges and the crucible of much of the state's rich cultural heritage, stitches together a collection of fascinating sights and experiences in the rarely explored central belt of Kerala between Kochi and Kozhikode. Busy Thrissur, the state's cultural capital, is unmissable in April and May when it holds its annual Pooram festival and millions pack into the city's central square, sardine-style, to watch the elephant procession and fireworks display. Coastal Guruvayur, meanwhile, is among Kerala's most sacred Hindu pilgrimage spots; it is home to one of India's wealthiest temples as well as an elephant yard where huge tuskers and their mahouts relax before they hit the road for the next festival. Inland, the Palakkad Gap cuts a broad trench through the Western Ghats, the only natural break in the mountain chain, providing a ready conduit for roads, railway lines, innumerable waves of historical migrants, and blasts of scorching air from the roasted plains of Tamil Nadu. Palakkad itself is now known as Kerala's granary, and makes a good stopover point on the route to or from Tamil Nadu.

Kerala's cultural capital with the state's most extravagant festival

Thrissur (population 317,500) sits at the west end of the Palakkad Gap, which runs through the low pass between the Nilgiri and the Palani hills. The route through the ghats is not scenic but it has been the most important link to the peninsula interior since Roman times. Thrissur is built round a hill on which stand the Vadakkunnathan Temple and an open green, which form the centre of the earth-shaking festivities. The town's bearings are given in cardinal directions from this raised 'Round'.

Vadakkunnathan Temple

Open 0400-1030, 1700-2030, non-Hindus not permitted inside except during the Pooram festival.

A predominantly Siva temple, is also known as the Rishabhadri or Thenkailasam ('Kailash of the South'). At the shrine to the Jain Tirthankara Vrishabha, worshippers offer a thread from their clothing, symbolically to cover the saint's nakedness. The shrine to Sankara Narayana has superb murals depicting stories from the *Mahabharata*. It is a classic example of the Kerala style of architecture with its special pagoda-like roof richly decorated with fine woodcarving.

The temple plays a pivotal role in the **Pooram** celebrations, held during April and May. This magnificent eight-day cacophony of a festival is marked by colourful processions joined by people of all religious groups irrespective of caste. Platoons of elephants decked out in gold, palm leaves and lamps march to the Vadakkunnathan Temple carrying priests and idols, to the accompaniment of dozens of drums, cymbals and pipes. On the final day temple teams meet on the Tekkinkadu maidan for a showdown of drumming and *Kudumattam* (the name roughly translates as 'umbrella swapping' – one of Kerala's more surreal spectator sports) before a huge fireworks display brings proceedings to a close. In September and October, there are live performances of *Chakyarkothu*, a classical art form. There is a small elephant compound attached to the temple.

Other sights

The **Town Hall** is a striking building housing an art gallery with murals from other parts of the state. In the **Archaeological Museum** ⓘ *Town Hall Rd, Tue-Sun 0900-1500*, ask to see

Essential Thrissur, Palakkad and the River Nila

Finding your feet

Trains on the main north–south line stop in Thrissur and Shoranur Junction, a handy jumping-off point for the River Nila. Trains from Kerala to Coimbatore and Chennai call at Palakkad. There are bus connections from these towns to the smaller centres, though to properly explore the cultural and historical riches of the area it's much more efficient to hire a guide and driver. See Transport, page 107.

the royal chariot. Next door, the **Art Museum** has woodcarvings, sculptures, an excellent collection of traditional lamps and old jewellery. Nearby, **Thrissur Zoo** ① *Tue-Sun 1000-1700, small fee*, is known for its snake collection. The impressive **Lourdes Church** has an interesting underground shrine.

Guruvayur

As one of the holiest sites in Kerala, Guruvayur, 29 km west of Thrissur, is a heaving pilgrimage centre, filled with stalls and thronged from 0300 to 2200 with people wanting to take *darshan* of Guruvayurappan.

Sri Krishna Temple The 16th-century Sri Krishna Temple is one of the richest in India, and there is a waiting list for the auspicious duty of lighting its oil lamps that stretches to 2025.

On well-augured marriage days there is a scrum in which couples are literally shunted from the podium by new pairs urgently pressing behind them in the queue, and the whole town is geared towards the wedding industry. The temple has an outer enclosure where there is a tall gold-plated flagpost and a pillar of lamps. The sanctum sanctorum is in the two-storeyed srikoil, with the image of the four-armed Krishna garlanded with pearls and marigolds. Photography of the tank is not allowed. Non-Hindus are not allowed inside and are not made to feel welcome.

Tip...
Devotees of the Sri Krishna Temple aren't afraid to put their money where their mouths are: in one month alone the temple can earn as much as Rs 11 million, along with just short of 4 kg of gold and almost 14 kg of silver.

Guruvayur Devaswom Institute of Mural Painting ① *Mon-Fri 1000-1600*. The temple's inner sanctum is off limits to non-Hindus, but you can visit this tiny educational institute where you can meet and buy finished works from the next generation of mural painters. As with *Kathakali*, the age-old decorative arts of temple culture steadily declined during the 20th century under the weakening structure of feudalism and opposition to the caste system. When the temple lost three walls to a fire in 1970 there were hardly any artists left to carry out renovation, prompting authorities to build the school in 1989. Today the small institute runs a five-year course on a scholarship basis for just 10 students. Paintings sell for Rs 500-15,000 depending on size, canvas, wood, etc.

Punnathur Kotta Elephant Yard ① *0900-1700, bathing 0900-0930, Rs 25, take care as elephants can be dangerous, buses from Thrissur (45 mins)*. Situated within a fort 4 km northwest of town, temple elephants (68 at the last count) are looked after here and wild ones are trained. There are some interesting insights into traditional animal training but this is not everyone's cup of tea. Though captive, the elephants are dedicated to Krishna and appear to be well cared for by their attendants. The elephants are donated by pious Hindus but religious virtue doesn't come cheap: the elephants cost Rs 500,000 each.

Kodungallur and around

At one time Kodungallur, 50 km southwest of Trichur on the border of Ernakulam District, was the west coast's major port, and the capital of the Chera king Cheraman Perumal.

Nearby **Kottapuram** is where St Thomas is believed to have landed in AD 52. The commemorative shrine was built in 1952. Kodungallur is also associated by tradition with the arrival of the first Muslims to reach India by sea. Malik-ibn-Dinar is reputed to have built India's first Juma Masjid, 2 km from town. Tiruvanchikulam Temple and the Portuguese fort are worth visiting. The Syrian Orthodox church in **Azikode** blends early Christian architecture in Kerala with surrounding Hindu traditions. Thus the images of Peter and Paul are placed where the *dvarapalas* (doorkeepers) of Hindu temples would be found, and the portico in front of the church is for pilgrims.

Listings Thrissur (Trichur) and around

Tourist information

Thrissur

DTPC Thrissur
Palace Rd, T0487-232 0800,
www.dtpcthrissur.com.

Guruvayur

DTPC Guruvayur
Vyjayanti Building, East Nada,
Guruvayur, T0487-255 0400.

Where to stay

Thrissur
Reserve ahead for Pooram, when prices rocket.

$$$$-$$$ Kadappuram Beach Resort
Nattika Beach, southwest of
Thrissur, T0487-239 4988, www.
kadappurambeachresorts.com.
Self-contained complex of bungalows and cottages in traditional Kerala design, but the emphasis here is on the Ayurveda and most come for the 14-day *panchakarma*. The Ayurveda centre is functional and not luxurious, but massage and medical attention are excellent. After treatments, cross the pretty river to a huge garden of coconut trees and hammocks that separates the hotel from the sea.

$$ Luciya Palace
Marar Rd, T0487-242 4731,
www.hotelluciyapalace.com.
35 rooms, 15 a/c, and 2 suites. Large, clean and quiet rooms, TV, garden restaurant, internet next door, good service, very pleasant hotel.

$ Bini Tourist Home
Round North, T0487-233 5703,
www.binitouristhome.com.
24 rooms, TV, shower, 10 a/c, basic but clean and spacious rooms, restaurant, bar.

$ Railway Retiring Rooms
Well looked after and very good value.

Guruvayur

$$$-$$ Krishna Inn
East Nada, Guruvayur, T0487-255 0777,
www.krishnainn.in.
Glossy hotel with white marble floors and spacious. 24-hr coffee shop, vegetarian, multi-cuisine **Thulasi** restaurant.

$$ Hotel Gokulam Vanamala
South Nada, Guruvayur, T0487-255 5213.
Popular with domestic tourists,
very clean rooms with big beds
and TV, telephone and hot water.
A/c, vegetarian restaurant (Keralite
food, 0600-2300), laundry.

$$ Mayura Residency
West Nada, Guruvayur, T0487-255 7174,
www.hotelmayuraguruvayur.com.
65 good-value, well-appointed rooms
in high-rise hotel with excellent views
from its rooftop. 24-hr coffee shop,
Amrutham vegetarian (continental,
South or North Indian) restaurant.

Restaurants

Most $ hotels have good restaurants,
particularly Siddhartha Regency's
Golden Fork, on Veliyannur Rd near
the station. In general, though, eating
out is still somewhat frowned on by
the traditional Brahmin families of
Kerala, so most eating options are
down-at-heel *dhabas*.

Thrissur

$$ City Centre
Next to Priya Tourist Home.
Western snacks, bakery and good
supermarket.

$$ Navaratna
Naduvilal, Round West, T0487-242 1994.
Open 1000-2300.
Pure vegetarian North Indian restaurant
divided into booths.

$ Elite Bharat
Chembottil Lane.
Good honest Keralan and South Indian
food – *dosas, puttu, thalis* – served
without ceremony to huge crowds
of locals.

$ Sapphire
Railway Station Rd. Open 0630-2200.
Excellent lime green and stone eatery
dishing up *thalis* and the best chicken
biryanis in town.

Festivals

Thrissur
Jan-Feb Several temple festivals
involving elephants are held in
the surrounding villages which
can be as rewarding as **Pooram**
(eg **Koorkancherry Thaippoya
Mahotsavam**, or **Thaipooya
Kavadiyattam**, held at Sri Maheswara
Temple, Koorkancherry, 2 km from
Thrissur). Also held at the end of Feb is
the **Uthralikavu Pooram**, at its most
colourful at the Sri Ruthura Mahakalikavu
Temple, Parithipra, Vodakancherry, en
route to Shornur Junction.
End Mar 7-day **Arratupuzha Festival**
at the Ayappa Temple, 14 km from
Thrissur. On the 5th day the deity
parades with 9 decorated elephants,
while on the 6th day **Pooram** is
celebrated on a grand scale with
61 elephants in the temple grounds.
Apr-May The magnificent 8-day
Pooram, a grand festival with elephants,
parasols, drums and fireworks, should
not be missed. Several temples in
town participate but particularly the
Thiruvambady and Paramekkavu.
It is marked by very noisy, colourful
processions, joined by people from all
religious groups, irrespective of caste.
The festivities are held 1300-1700
and again at night from around 2000.
Elaborately bedecked elephants (each
temple allowed up to 15) specially
decorated with lamps and palm
leaves, march to the Vadakkunnathan
Temple carrying priests and deities to

the accompaniment of extraordinary drumming. On the final day temple teams meet on the Tekkinkadu *maidan* for the drumming and *Kudumattam* competition; the festival terminates with a huge display of fireworks. **Aug/Sep Kamdassamkadavu Boat Races** at Onam. Also performances of **Pulikali**, unique to Thrissur, when mimers dressed as tigers dance to drumbeats.

Guruvayur
The following festivals take place at Punnathur Kotta, 4 km out of town. **Feb/Mar Utsavam**, 10 days of festivities start with an elephant race and continue with colourful elephant processions and performances of *Krishnanattom* dances. Details from Kerala tourist offices. **Nov-Dec** 5-day **Ekadasi** with performances of *Krishnanattom*, a forerunner of *Kathakali* – an 8-day drama cycle.

Bus There are yellow-top local buses available. For long distance, there are 3 bus stands. **KSRTC**, near railway station, T0487-242 1842, southwest of 'Round', including several to **Alappuzha** (3½ hrs), **Bengaluru** (10 hrs), **Coimbatore** (3 hrs), **Guruvayur** (1 hr), **Kochi** (2 hrs), **Kozhikode**, **Chennai** (13 hrs), **Palakkad** and **Thiruvananthapuram** (7 hrs). **North (Priyadarshini)**, just north of 'Round', buses to **Cheruthuruthy**, **Ottapalam**, **Palakkad**. Sakthan Thampuran, 2 km south of 'Round', for frequent private buses to **Guruvayur**, **Kannur**, **Kozhikode**.

Train Enquiries, T0487-242 3150. All trains connecting Kochi with points north stop in Thrissur. **Ernakulam**: more than 20 trains a day, 1¼ hrs. **Chennai**: *Chennai Mail 12624*, 2040, 10½ hrs. **Bengaluru**: *Bangalore Intercity Exp 12678*, 1020, 9½ hrs. **Mangalore**: *Parasuram Exp 16650*, 1240, 7½ hrs (via **Kozhikode**, 3 hrs).

North of Thrissur the road and railway cut through lush countryside of paddy fields, quiet villages and craggy red hills mantled with coconut and rubber plantations, before crossing the wide sandy bed of the Bharatapuzha River at Shoranur. Known to the people who populate its banks as Nila, this is Kerala's longest river, rising on the eastern side of the Palakkad Gap and winding lazily through 209 km to spill into the Arabian Sea at the bustling fishing port of Ponnani.

Though its flow is severely depleted by irrigation dams and its bed gouged by sand miners, the importance of the river to Kerala's cultural development is hard to overstate: Ayurveda, *Kathakali* (see box, page 81) and the martial art *Kalaripayattu* were all nurtured along the banks of the Nila, not to mention the cacophonous classical music that soundtracks festive blow-outs like the Thrissur **Pooram**. Folk tradition too is vibrantly represented: elaborately adorned devotees carry colourful effigies to temple festivals, snake worshippers roam house to house performing ancient rituals to seek blessing from the serpent gods, and village musicians sing songs of the paddy field mother goddess, passed down from generation to generation.

Despite all this, the Nila thus far remains refreshingly untouched by Kerala's tourism boom, and few travellers see more of it than the glimpses afforded by the beautiful train ride between Shoranur and Kozhikode. This is in part because there's little tourist infrastructure, few genuine 'sights', and no easy way for a travellers to hook into the cultural scene. Traditional potters and brass-smiths labour in humble workshops behind unmarked houses, while performers (singers and dancers by night, coolies, plumbers and snack sellers by day) only get together for certain events. With your own transport you can search out any number of beautiful riverside temples, but unless you join one of the superb storytelling tours run by local guiding outfit **The Blue Yonder** (see page 110), Kerala Kalamandalam (see below) might be the only direct contact you have with the Nila's rich heritage.

Kerala Kalamandalam

3 km south of river, Cheruthuruthy, south of Shoranur Junction, T04884-262305, www.kalamandalam.org, Mon-Fri 0930-1300, closed public holidays and Apr-May. Frequent private buses from Thrissur's northern bus stand (ask for Vadakkancheri Bus Stand) go straight to Kalamandalam, taking about 1 hr.

This residential school is dedicated to preserving the state's unique forms of performance art. Founded in 1930, after the provincial rulers' patronage for the arts dwindled in line with their plummeting wealth and influence, the Kalamandalam spear-headed a revival of *Kathakali* dancing, along with *ottam thullal* and the all-female drama *mohiniyattam*. The school and the state tourism department run a fascinating three-hour tour of the campus, 'A Day With the Masters' (US$25), with in-depth explanations of the significance and background of the art forms, the academy and its architecture, taking you through the various open air *kalaris* (classrooms) to watch training sessions. There are all-night *Kathakali* performances on 26 January, 15 August, and 9 November. *Koodiyattam*, the oldest surviving form of Sanskrit theatre, is enshrined by UNESCO as an 'oral and intangible heritage of humanity'.

Ponnani

In the bustling port town of Ponnani at the mouth of the Nila, the **Ponnani Juma Masjid** ⓘ *42 km northwest of Thrissur, nearest train station 21 km away at Kuttipuram; admission to non-Muslims not assured, dress conservatively, women should wear a headscarf*, was built in the mid-15th century by the spiritual leader Zainudhin Ibn Ali Ibn Ahmed Ma'bari, who employed a Hindu carpenter to design the exterior. Ignorant of traditional Islamic architecture, the carpenter carved the elaborate teak-wood façade to resemble a Hindu temple incorporating many intricate Hindu designs. The carpenter was killed by a fall from the roof as he finished construction and lies buried inside the mosque. The nearby fishing docks are a hive of activity, but prepare for plenty of attention from local boys.

Listings Along the River Nila

Where to stay

$$$$-$$$ River Retreat
Palace Rd, Cheruthuruthy, T0488-426 2244, www.riverreatreat.in.
Heritage hotel and Ayurvedic resort in the former (and much-extended) home of the maharajas of Kochi. Spacious rooms have a/c, TV and modern baths, great views onto large tree-filled garden that backs onto the Nila. Period furniture adds a nice touch to the airy communal areas. Tours of the local area, restaurant, bar, pool, Wi-Fi.

$$$ Ayurveda Mana
Peringode, via Kootanadu, T0487-256 0228, www.poomullyayurvedamana.com.
Authentic Ayurveda centre set in a fascinating 600-year-old *illam*, with treatments following the traditional methods of Poomully Aram Thampuran, a renowned expert in the discipline. Quiet airy rooms (all with TV) open onto shady veranda and peaceful manicured grounds. Full range of health care treatments available and specialized therapies for arthritis, sports injuries, infertility, etc. All treatments include individually assessed diet, massage and medicine.

$$$ Maranat Mana
Old Ooty–Mysore Rd, Pandikkad (an hour's drive north of Pattambi), T0493-128 6252, www.maranatmana.com.
Special homestay in a traditional *namboodhiri* (Kerala Brahmin) household. Hosts Praveen and Vidya have sensitively converted the 160-year-old guesthouse attached to their ancestral home into 3 cool and airy rooms, all with fans and modern baths. You can visit the sprawling main family residence, one of the last surviving examples of Keralite *pathinaru kettu* ('four courtyards') architecture, which contains a Ganesh shrine to which devotees flock from far and wide. Delicious vegetarian meals included,

and local tours, Ayurvedic treatments, yoga classes, cultural activities can be arranged. Fascinating and highly recommended, reservations essential.

$$$ Olappamanna Mana
Vellinezhi, T0466-228 5797, www.olappamannamana.com.
Majestic manor house, in rosewood, teak and jackfruit trees, to the highest Keralite Hindu caste of *namboodris*, parts of which date back 3 centuries. Pure vegetarian cuisine, no alcohol, 6 bedrooms, with bathroom and fan, no a/c.

What to do

If you're in search of Ayurvedic healing at its most authentic and traditional, the River Nila and Palakkad regions, far inland from the pore-clogging salt air coming off the Arabian Sea, are the best places in Kerala to find it. But don't come here expecting 5-star spa masseurs who'll tiptoe around your Western foibles about comfort and bodily privacy. These treatments are administered to you in the almost-raw, on hard wooden beds amid buckets of oil – and when your treatment is over your torturer may accompany you to the shower to make sure you thoroughly degrease.

Body and soul
Arya Vaidya Sala, *Kottakal town, T0483-274 3380, www.aryavaidyasala.com.*
One of the biggest and best Ayurvedic centres in India, with a fully equipped hospital offering 4-week *panchkarma* treatments as well as on-site medicine factory and research department.

Tour operators
The Blue Yonder, *T0413-450 2218, www.theblueyonder.com.* Award-winning responsible travel tour operator, focused on conserving local culture and traditions. Tours are carried out in a way that allows travellers to become fully immersed in the region's folk traditions and fables, and travelling here can feel like being in the Arabian Nights. Flexible, individual itineraries can include homestays, cultural performances, monsoon rafting in self-built bamboo-and-inner-tube rafts, backwater cruises, legend and heritage trails. Heartily recommended.

area of verdant plains, known for its Brahmin villages and paddy fields

Kerala's rice cellar, prosperous Palakkad (population 130,700) has long been of strategic importance for its gap – the only break in the mountain ranges that otherwise block the state from Tamil Nadu and the rest of India. Whereas once this brought military incursions, today the gap bears tourist buses from Chennai and tractors for the rich agricultural fields here. Few educated modern Keralites care to plough using the old bullock carts (although the tradition is kept alive through *kaalapoottu*, a series of races between yoked oxen held in mud-churned paddy fields every January). The name Palakkad comes from *pala*, a type of tree, and *kadu*, which means forest; the area was once thickly covered in forests of this type, but these have long been usurped by paddy fields.

Palakkad Fort
The region is filled with old architecture of *illams* and *tharavadus* belonging to wealthy landowners making a visit worthwhile in itself – but chief among the actual sights is Palakkad Fort, a granite structure in Palakkad town itself, built by Haider Ali in 1766, and taken over by the British in 1790. It now has a Hanuman temple inside. Ask directions locally to the 500-year-old Jain temple of **Jainimedu** in the town's western suburbs, a 10-m-long granite temple with Jain *Thirthankaras* and *Yakshinis* built for the Jain sage Chandranathaswami. Only one Jain family is left in the region, but the area around this temple is one of the only places in Kerala where remnants of the religion have survived.

Kalpathy
Also well worth visiting in the region are the many traditional **Brahmin villages**: Kalpathy, 10 km outside Palakkad, holds the oldest Siva temple in Malabar, dating from AD 1425 and built by Kombi Achan, then Raja of Palakkad. But the village itself, an 800-year-old settlement by a self-contained Tamil community, is full of beautiful houses with wooden shutters and metal grills and is now a World Heritage Site that gives you a glimpse of village life that has been held half-frozen in time for nearly 1000 years. The temple here is called **Kasiyil Pakuthi Kalpathy** meaning Half Banares because its situation on the river is reminiscent of the Banares temple on the Ganges. A 10-day **car festival** in November centres on this temple and features teak chariots tugged by people and pushed by elephants.

Nelliyampathy
56 km from Palakkad town.

This hill station, with a tiny community of planters, is famous for its oranges, but there are also orchids, bison, elephant and butterflies in abundance. The view across the Keralite plains from Seethakundu is stunning; a third of the district lies spread out under you. The area has good trekking, too.

Ramassery Iddli

Another unique feature of Palakkad is the *Ramassery Iddli* made at the Sarswathy tea stall, daily 0500-1830, iddli Rs 1.50, chai Rs 2.50. If you spend any time on the street in South India, your morning meal will inevitably feature many of these tasty steamed fermented rice cakes. Palakkad is home to a peculiar take on the dumpling, one that has been developed to last for days rather than having to be cooked from fresh. The four families in this poky teashop churn out 5000 *iddlis* a day. Originally settlers from somewhere near Coimbatore, in Tamil Nadu, over 100 years ago, they turned to making this variety of *iddli* when there wasn't enough weaving work to sustain their families. They started out selling them door to door, but pretty soon started to get orders for weddings. The *iddlis* are known to have travelled as far afield as Delhi, by plane in a shipment of 300. Manufacturers have started to arrive in order to buy the secret recipe.

Megalith trail: Guruvayur to Kunnamkulam

The Palakkad Gap has been one of the few relatively easy routes through the ghats for 3000 years and this area is noted for its megalithic monuments. Megalithic cultures spread from the Tamil Nadu plains down into Kerala, but developed local forms. The small villages of Eyyal, Chovvanur, Kakkad, Porkalam, Kattakampala and Kadamsseri, between Guruvayur and Kunnamkulam, have hoodstones, hatstones, dolmens, burial urns and *menhirs*.

Listings Palakkad (Palghat)

Tourist information

Palakkad DTPC
West Fort Rd, Palakkad, T0491-253 8996,
www.dtpcpalakkad.com.

Where to stay

$$$$ Kalari Kovilakom
Kollengode, T0492-326 3155,
www.kalarikovilakom.com.
The Maharani of Palakkad's 1890 palace has been restored to make this extremely disciplined yet very luxurious Ayurvedic retreat: the indulgence of a palace meets the austerity of an ashram. Treatments include anti-ageing, weight loss, stress management and ailment healing. Lessons include yoga, meditation, Ayurvedic cookery. Strictly no exertion (no sunbathing or swimming). No mod cons (TV, etc), bar, internet. Minimum stay of 14 days.

$$$ Kairali Ayurvedic Health Resort
Kodumbu, T0492-322 2553, www.
ayurvedichealingvillage.com.
The 3-day packages at this excellent resort offer an easy entry to Ayurveda. Beautifully landscaped grounds include a dairy and farm, pool and tennis courts.

$$$ Kandath Tharavad
Thenkurussi, T0492-228 4124,
www.tharavad.info.
A magical place tucked away in
Palakkad's fields, 6 rooms in a 200-year-
old mud and teak ancestral home
with natural dyed floor tiles of ochre,
terracotta and blue. Nadumuttams open
out onto the stars and doors are thick
wedges of teak and brass. Bagwaldas,
your gracious host, will guide you
through local customs and culture as
engagingly as he steers you through the
physical landscape.

$$-$ Fort Palace
West Fort Rd, Palakkad, T0491-253 4621,
www.fortpalace.com. Rs 1500-3400
(plus taxes).
19 rooms, groovy old-style hotel some
good a/c, restaurant, brash mock
turrets. Satellite TV and hot water.
Continental/Indian food in restaurant,
and bar, both gloomy and packed
(lawn service). Nice shared sit-out on
1st floor, spotless, large double beds.
Chandeliers, wood panelling.

$$-$ Indraprastha
English Church Rd, Palakkad, T0491-253
4641, www.hotelindraprastha.com.
Rs 1700-4000 (plus taxes).
Kitsch and cool: 30 rooms in 1960s block,
dark wood, leather banquettes and
bronze lettering. Dark bar permanently
packed, lawn service, 24-hr vegetarian
coffee shop, exchange, internet,
bookshop. Multi-cuisine restaurant.

$ Garden House (KTDC)
Malampuzha, T0491-281 5217, www.
ktdc.com. Rs 1250-1800 (plus taxes).

17 somewhat chintzy rooms in a 1-star
government restaurant on hilltop
overlooking the Malampuzha Dam,
a popular picnic spot. Mostly non-a/c
rooms, pleasant.

Restaurants

Be sure to try an *iddli* from the
Sarswarthy tea stall, see box, opposite.

$ Ashok Bhavan
GB Rd, Palakkad.
Modest vegetarian South Indian snacks.

$ Hotel Noor Jehan
GB Rd, Palakkad, T0491-252 2717.
Non-vegetarian a/c restaurant that
specializes in *moplah biryani* and *pathiri*,
rice chappatis.

$ KR Bakes
Palakkad. Open 0900-2300.
Puffs, ice creams, *halva* plus juice bar
and savoury meals after 1600.

Transport

Bus **KSRTC**, buses run from
the **Municipal Bus Stand**, T0491-
252 7298, www.keralartc.com,
to **Coimbatore**, **Kozhikode**,
Mannarghat (Silent Valley), **Pollachi**.

Train The main **Junction station**,
T0491-255 5231, is 5 km northeast of
town. Some passenger trains also stop
at the more central **Town station**. To
Coimbatore: frequent trains all day,
1-1½ hrs, some continue to **Chennai**
or **Bengaluru**. To Ernakulam (**Kochi**):
many trains, 2½ hrs, all go via **Thrissur**,
1-2 hrs. To **Mangalore**:, 9 hrs, via
Kozhikode, 4 hrs.

Malabar

The Malabar region is the unsung jewel of Kerala: the combination of the state's political administration in the south plus the pious Muslim community and orthodoxy of the Hindu population have made it more resistant to tourist development than the more easy-going Catholic-influenced stretch south from Kochi. Any cohesion between north and south Kerala is political, not cultural: Malabar was under the Madras Presidency before Independence, lumped together with the Travancore south only in 1956. The atmosphere couldn't be more different. The coastal towns of Kozhikode (formerly Calicut), Thalassery and Kannur are strongholds of the Muslim Moplah community, whose long-standing trading links with the Middle East have bred a deep cultural affinity that's reflected in the lime-green houses lining the roads and the increasing number of women seen in purdah. At the same time, Malabar is one of the best places to see Kerala's Hindu religious and cultural traditions in their proper context: *Theyyam* (the ritual temple dance that spawned *Kathakali*) and *Kalaripayattu* (the stunning martial art) are both practised here. Inland from Kozhikode, the glorious hilltop district of Wayanad experiences some of the heaviest rainfall in the world, and its familiar stubble of tea plantations is interspersed with some of the most stunning and accessible rainforest in the state.

Kozhikode (population 436,500) is a major commercial centre for northern Kerala and the centre for Kerala's timber industry; it is also dependent on the petro-dollar, as testified by the scores of direct flights to the Gulf each day. Around 1.2 million Keralites work in the Gulf, generating revenue of about US$12 billion for Kerala. It's also a jumping-off point for Wayanad.

The city itself is engaged in mostly small-scale retail. Off the brash and crowded main boulevard, tiny lanes thread between high laterite walls with everything happening on the street. Remnants of the spice trade remain and the markets are great. Court Road is home to pepper, the black gold that lured Vasco, as well as copra and coconut oil. There are beautiful wooden mosques built like Hindu temples, and in nearby Beypore, where the Chaliyar river meets the Arabian Sea, you still have half a chance of watching the birth of an *uru* – the massive deep-sea hauler-sized wooden boats that have been built by Muslim Khalasi shipbuilders with few technological changes since Cheraman Perumal ordered one for a trip to Arabia in the sixth century.

Kuttichera

The Sunni Muslim quarter of Kuttichera, behind the railway station to the west of town, holds several fascinating multi-tiered **wooden mosques,** set around a huge green pond to which flocks of white-capped elders gather in the late afternoon. Legend has it that a ghost within the pond seizes a human sacrifice each year, releasing the body after three days. The mosques date from the 15th century and bear a puzzlingly close resemblance to Hindu temple structures. **Mishkal Masjid** is one of the oldest, and was named for the wealthy trader who built it, but also look for **Jami Masjid** and **Munchunthi Palli**. The latter has a 13th-century *vattezhuthu* (inscribed slab of stone) that proclaims the donation of the land to the mosque by a Zamorin. Women should cover their head, shoulders and limbs in this area.

Note the size of the houses around here, which are known to accommodate more than 150 family members each. The *puyappala* tradition (literally translates as 'fresh husband') means that each marrying daughter takes the husband back into her parents' home. One house is supposed to have 300 people living under the same roof: each building has an average of three kitchens.

From here you can walk along Beach Road, where crumbling old buildings that were once trading centres are now being busily demolished. The beach itself is more of a town latrine than a place for swimming.

Essential Kozhikode (Calicut)

Finding your feet

Karipur airport, 25 km south, has connections with the Middle East as well as several major Indian cities. The station and main bus stand are on opposite sides of the town centre, both within easy reach of several hotels. Autos are widely available and surprisingly cheap. See Transport, page 118.

East Hill

The **Pazhassiraja Museum** ⓘ *5 km north of the centre on East Hill, Tue-Sun 0900-1630, Rs 10,* has copies of original murals plus bronzes, old coins and models of the some of the area's megalithic monuments. Next door is the **art gallery**, with an excellent collection of paintings by Indian artists as well as wood and ivory carvings, and the **Krishna Menon Museum** ⓘ *Mon and Wed, 1000-1230, 1430-1700, free,* dedicated to the Keralite politician who became a leading left-wing figure in India's post-Independence Congress government.

Around Kozhikode

Kappad, 16 km north, and now the site of a poor, mainly Muslim fishing village, is where Vasco da Gama and his 170 sailors landed on 27th May 1498. There is an old plaque by the approach road to the beach commemorating the event. Although it is a pleasant spot, the sea is unsuitable for swimming since pollution

Kozhikode (Calicut)

To Ballussery
To Kannur
To Wynad
Pazhassiraja Museum, Wynad Rd
Art Gallery & Krishna
Menon Museum
Civil Station
Co-op
Bypass Rd
Vellayil
Railway
Station
Kannur Rd
Gandhi Rd
Joseph Rd
Bank R
Lions
Park
Lighthouse
Vellayil Rd
Customs Rd
P T Usha Rd
KSRTC
6
2
4
1
Indira Gandhi Rd (Mavoor Rd)
New DC Books
Bus Stand
2
3
To Mavoor
Government
Red Cross Rd
CSI
Beach Rd
Corporation Rd
Convent Rd
Bank Rd
AG Rd
Cherooty Rd
3
Manachira
Comtrust
Pavamani Rd
Puthiyara Rd
Rajaji Rd
Court Rd
Railway Station Rd
Taxis
5
Taxis
MP Rd
Big Bazar R
Palayam Rd
Veg
1
Palayam
Bus Stand
M M Ali Rd (Jail Rd)
P T NZ
Link Rd
Tuli Temple
To 2
To Airport (25 km) & Thrissur

N
400 metres (approx)
400 yards (approx)

Where to stay 🛏
Alakapuri Guest House 1
Arora Tourist Home 2
Asma Tower 3

Hyson Heritage 4
Malabar Palace 5
Metro Tourist Home 6

Restaurants 🍴
Dakshin 1
Sagar 2
Zain's 3

from Kozhikode filters down this far and the beach itself is used as a toilet by the fishermen.

Beypore, half an hour south of Calicut, was once a significant port, but is now famous only for its boatyard, where families of Khalasis have used traditional methods to make *urus* (huge wooden vessels) for 1500 years. The wiry Khalasis craft the ships using memorized plans and ancient construction techniques, now mainly for the benefit of wealthy Arab clients who deploy them as luxury yachts or floating restaurants.

Listings Kozhikode (Calicut) *map p116*

Tourist information

Kerala Tourism
Railway Station, T0495-270 2606,
www.dtpckozhikode.com.
Has limited information about the town. The branch at the railway station hands out brochures on North Kerala and can help with hotel bookings.

Where to stay

$$$ Harivihar Ayurvedic Heritage Home
Bilathikulam, T0495-276 5865,
www.harivihar.com.
In Calicut's pretty Brahminical suburbs, this immaculate former royal home is surrounded by lawns with giant mango and jackfruit trees and a beautiful green water tank where you can undertake pukka Ayurveda or study Indian philosophy, Sanskrit, vasthu and yoga in a small guesthouse setting run by conventional medics. You can also stay on a B&B basis, in one of 5 doubles and 3 singles. Gentle Sivananda yoga, Ayurveda from Coimbatore Arya Vaidya Pharmacy, no alcohol.

$$$ Tasara
Calicut–Beypore Rd, Beypore, T0495-
241 4832, www.tasaraindia.com.
A weaving centre amid a garden of mango and jackfruit trees. Rooms with fan and basic bath. Vasudevan, Balakrishnan and their sisters have been running textile workshops here since 1979, and guests come to take courses in weaving, block-printing, batik, silkscreen and natural dyeing. Price includes all meals, tuition and activities. Good discounts for monthly stays, reservations essential.

$$$-$$ Malabar Palace
GH Rd, Manuelsons' Junction, T0495-
272 1511, www.malabarpalacecalicut.
com. Rs 3200-4750 (plus taxes).
52 a/c rooms, excellent a/c restaurant, bar, very helpful reception.

$$ Alakapuri
Moulana Mohammed Ali Rd,
T0495-272 3451. Bar 1000-2200,
dining hall 0700-2200.
40 rooms set around a charming garden brimming with plants and trees and lotus pond. Simple, spacious, with old furniture, phone, tubs and TV. Dates from 1958, and easily Calicut's most characterful mid-range option.

$$ Hotel Asma Tower
Mavoor Rd, T0495-272 3560,
www.asmatower.com.
44 a/c and non-a/c rooms in gleaming
new tower. Inside, expect 2-tone mint
green decor, frosty a/c system, perfumed
air, muzak and TV and telephone in
every room. Good value.

$$-$ Hyson Heritage
114 Bank Rd, T0495-276 6423,
www.hysonheritage.com.
A breezy, efficient and well-maintained
business hotel, with 89 spotless, smallish
rooms with phone, cable TV, bath, 47 a/c,
set around a large courtyard. Ayurvedic
treatments available.

$ Arora Tourist Home
Railway Station Rd, T0495-230 6889.
Not as ship-shape as the outside and
ground floor suggest, but the huge,
cheap rooms here are OK if you just
want to dump your bags after a train
ride. Street noise dies down overnight,
but mosquitoes don't rest.

$ Metro Tourist Home
Mavoor Rd Junction, T0495-276 6582.
42 pleasing rooms, some with TV, a bit
noisy, South Indian restaurant. Gloomy
with grubby paintwork but clean sheets,
big mirrors and good fans.

$ Railway Retiring Rooms
Very spacious, clean, good service.

Restaurants

$$ Malabar Palace
See Where to stay.
International, a/c, excellent food
and service.

$ Dakshin
17/43 Mavoor Rd. Open 0630-2230.

Dead cheap place for *dosa*, pizza, cutlet
and curd rice (meals from Rs 15).

$ Hotel Sagar
5/3305 Mavoor Rd, T0495-272 5058.
Open 0530 onwards.
So popular they've launched their
own hotel, and another restaurant (the
original is already multistorey). Sagar is
famous for its biriyanis, and also does
superb breakfasts of *dahl* and *parotta*.
Upstairs is for families and a/c rooms;
downstairs is the cattle class.

$ Zain's Hotel
Convent Cross Rd.
A simple place run by a Muslim husband
and wife. Mussels, biriyanis for Rs 30 and
fish curries for Rs 15.

Transport

Air Kozhikode Airport is 30 km south
of the city, T0495-271 9491. Domestic
flights to **Mumbai**, **Coimbatore**,
Goa, **Chennai**, and **Tiruchirapalli**.
International flights to **Abu Dhabi** (UAE),
Bahrain, **Doha**, Dubai, **Jeddah**, **Kuwait**,
Muscat, and **Sharjah** (UAE).

Bus KSRTC, T0495-272 3796, www.
keralartc.com, from bus stand on Mavoor
Rd (near Bank Rd junction) to **Bengaluru**,
Thiruvananthapuram (via Thrissur,
Ernakulam, Alappuzha, Kollam), 0630-2200
(10 hrs), **Ooty** (see Wayanad, page 124).
The **New Bus Stand**, T0495-272 2823,
is further east on Mavoor Rd for private
buses to the north including **Kannur**.
Local buses operate from **Palayam Bus
Stand** on Kallai Rd, T0495-272 0397.

Train Enquiries, T0495-270 1234. Trains
to **Chennai**, **Coimbatore**, **Ernakulam**
(4½ hrs) via **Shoranur** and **Thrissur**,
Goa, **Mangalore** (5 hrs), **Mumbai**,
Thiruvananthapuram (9½-10 hrs).

Mahé

The borders of the 9 sq km that make up French Kerala are marked not by baguette bakeries or pavement cafés, but by shops screaming 'Foreign Liquor'. By night, the 35,000 residents of this outpost of Pondicherry disappear to make way for the truckers who rush through to stock up on half-price whiskies and brandies, taking advantage of the colony's special tax status.

By day, however, Mahé is pretty enough: policemen wear French hats and the town is beautifully positioned on a slight hill overlooking the river. It was named after Mahé de Labourdonnais, who captured it for the French in 1725. Many people here still speak French and the very French **Church of St Theresa** celebrates its feast day on 14-15 October. The beaches to the south and north of town are dirty and are not safe for swimming due to undercurrents.

Thalassery (Tellicherry)

Like everywhere along the Malabar's increasingly gold coast, banks here double as pawnbrokers. Despite an obsession with wealth, at the wide, tree-covered street level you'll find a town that's friendly, brilliantly walkable and lined with 19th-century shops complete with original wooden cupboards and cobwebs. It's a town of cricket, cakes and circuses. Author Herman Hesse's mother was born here.

Sights
Fort area and around   Thalassery was set up by the British East India Company in 1683 to export pepper and cardamom. In 1708 they obtained permission to build a **fort** which, having survived a siege laid by Haidar Ali, is still standing today on a rocky promontory about 15 m above sea level. Its proud little gateway, raised on a flight of steps, is flanked by colourful mustachioed figures.

There are some attractive old buildings. The Armenian church is rather shabby now but the Catholic church still thrives though the population is largely *Moplah* (Kerala Muslims). The **Odathil Mosque**, believed to be 400 years old, is in the traditional Kerala style with a gabled roof and copper sheeting.

Mambally's Royal Biscuit Factory   ⓘ *Near the Old Police Station, T0490-232 1207, 0900-2030.* Established in 1880, claims to be where cake was first baked in Kerala. Nowadays you'll find jam rolls, ketchup, Nestlé milky bars and lime pickle along with the fresh bakes. The downstairs of the double-decker shops is crowded with hessian sacks full of cinnamon from China, cloves from Madagascar, raisins from Afghanistan and star anise from China and Vietnam. Some of the owners are third generation traders.

Fish market ① *0600-1800.* This is one of the liveliest fish markets in Kerala. Men with cleavers stand tall over barracudas and manta, while stacks of clams, mussels, shrimp and mackerel are constantly replenished with new loads. Fish are then sped along the state highway to reach markets in Kochin and Mangalore.

Kalaris and circus training Thalassery is also a centre for training in gymnastics and circus acts, so street performers and acrobats are not uncommon; 90% of India's circus companies originate here. You can see martial arts in local *kalaris*: one of the best being the tricky-to-find *kalari* of **K Viswanathan Gurukkal** ① *MKG Kalari Sangham, Kuzhippangad, PO Chirakkara, T0490-237110, call in advance.*

Muzhapilangad Beach Some 8 km from Thalassery, is nicknamed 'Drive In Beach'. It is an unspoilt, beautifully picturesque 4-km-long stretch of golden sand edged by palm trees at the northern end. Amazingly empty most of the time, it earned its nickname from the local custom of ragging trucks and Ambassadors up and down its firm sands.

Listings Thalassery (Tellicherry)

Where to stay

$$$$ Ayisha Manzil
Court Rd, T(0)9496-189296,
www.ayishamanzil.com. Rs 16,500
(including all taxes and meals).
A delightful mid-19th-century, colonial-style heritage home overlooking the sea. 6 huge a/c rooms with carved teak and rosewood furniture, massive baths, lots of British and Malabari memorabilia, amazing fresh seafood and cookery courses, temple pond pool, superb panoramic views, excursions.

$$-$ Hotel Pranam
AVK Nair Rd, Narangapuram,
T0490-232 0634.
14 cleanish rooms with bath – 4 with a/c, a little grubby. The a/c deluxe room has an extraordinary green carpeted sitting room attached.

$ Paris Presidency
New Paris Complex, Logan's Rd, T0490-234 2666, www.parispresidency.com.
Rs 1200-2200 (plus taxes).
24 clean and comfortable rooms with baths, TV, phone, restaurant, wood furniture, bright white walls in busy shopping area. Multi-cuisine restaurant.

Restaurants

$$ Ayisha Manzil
Court Rd, T(0)9496-189296.
Peerless homestay, serving food unlike you'll get anywhere outside a home. Phone for meals in advance.

$ Royal Visitors' Family Restaurant
Pranam Tourist Home, T0490-234 4292.
Open 0630-2300.
Grilled mussels, etc.

an agreeable town with good beaches, weaving and Theyyam rituals

Standing on raised ground with cliffs at the sea face, this town boasts a coconut-fringed coastline with some attractive beaches. Weavers' co-operatives and *beedi* factories provide employment but this is also a good place to watch *Theyyam* dances.

Fort area and around

The centre of the Moplah community (a group of Arab descent), Kannur was also the capital of the North Kolathiri Rajas for several hundred years. **Fort St Angelo** ⓘ *0900-1800* was built out of laterite blocks by the Portuguese in 1505 and taken over by the British in 1790 as their most important military base in the south. The picturesque **Moplah town** is round the bay to the south of the fort. The attractive **Payyambalam Beach** is 2 km away.

Kanhirode Weavers' Cooperative Society

Koodali Kannur, T0497-285 7259, 0900-1700, free.

Handloom weavers produce silk and cotton saris, shirts, *lungis* and soft furnishings sold through local cooperatives. Kanhirode Weavers' Cooperative was founded in 1952 on Gandhian principle, has a yearly turnover of Rs 150 million (US$3.7 million) and exports 95% of its pure handloom fabric to the UK for the Futon Bed Company. Spun cotton is shipped in from Coimbatore, and dyed in huge vats after which the cooperative's 450 staff are expected to feed bobbins through the high wooden looms fast enough to make 42 m within 3½ days for women, or three for men. While some weave, others feed the raw heaps of cotton from wire frames onto wheels to make thread – in the silk section they use bicycle wheels. The daily wage is Rs 100 (US$2.45), and apparently the co-op is having trouble recruiting more of the caste, who, as caste rules relax, are going for higher paid jobs elsewhere. A visit here is well worth the journey.

Listings Kannur (Cannanore)

Tourist information

DTPC
At the railway station, T0497-270 3121, www.dtpckannur.com.

Where to stay

$$$-$$ Mascot Beach Resort
Near Baby Beach, Burnassery, 2 km from the centre, T0497-270 8445, www.mascotresort.com.

Good rooms in high-rise business hotel overlooking the sea, residents-only pool, located in the quiet cantonment area (Ayurvedic centre attached).

$$ Costa Malabari
Near Adykadalaya Temple, 6 km south of town (by bus, ask to get out at Thazhe Chowwa), T0484-237 1761, www.touristdesk.in.
An unpretentious guesthouse converted from a warehouse with 4 rooms off a main hall. The owners have authored

a book on Kerala's festivals and have encyclopaedic knowledge of the local *Theyyam* scene. Difficult to get to and far from the centre, but there are 5 idyllic, wholly empty beaches within walking distance. Meals included.

$$-$ Royal Omars Thavakkara Kannur
Very close to the railway station and colourful market area, T0497-276 9091, http://www.royalomars.com.
Spanking new, with spacious standard non-a/c doubles at bargain rates. 60 rooms, TV, credit cards.

$ Hotel Savoy
Beach Rd, T0497-276 0074.
Bags of character in this super-clean, old-fashioned complex of bungalow cottages set around a lawn. A/c cottages are wonderfully spacious and cool. Bar attached.

Restaurants

$$ Chakara Drive in Restaurant
Cliff Exotel International, Payyabalam, T0497-271 2197.
Specials are sizzlers plus spicy fried *kallumakais* mussels and Malabar biriyani.

$ Indian Coffee House
Fort Rd.
For snacks.

$ Mascot Beach Resort's Restaurants
Near Baby Beach, Burnasseri, T0497-270 8445, www.mascotresort.com.
Some of the best top-end eating in town.

$ MVK Restaurant
SM Rd, T0497-276 7192. Open 1000-2200.
A local institution which has been packed from its opening 50 years ago, thanks to its commitment to fresh, home-ground spice mixes for its biriyanis, their rice

grains steeped in ghee. Serves beautiful, potent lime tea too.

$ Regency Snacks and Fast Food
Opposite Sangeetha Theatre, SN Park Rd.
Popular café with locals.

$ Your Choice Restaurant
Fort Rd.
Authentic Malabari food.

Entertainment

Theyyam dance
At **Parssinikadavu Temple**, 20 km north of Kannur, reached by bus. Performances (Dec-Mar) of ritual dance theatre at dawn (taxi essential) and often late afternoon to dusk. Pilgrims sometimes seek blessing from the principal dancer who may go into a trance after taking on the role of Mutthapan, a manifestation of Siva as Hunter.

What to do

PVA Ayurvedic Multi Speciality Nursing Home, *Onden Rd, T0497-276 0609, www.ayurvedaacharya.com.*
The down-at-heel PVA provides training courses in Ayurveda as well as rejuvenation, purification packages and direct treatments for ailments like disc prolapse, psoriasis and obesity. The 3 doctors here are highly regarded.

Transport

Bus Enquiries: T0497-270 7777. To **Kozhikode** (2½ hrs), **Mangalore** (4½ hrs), **Mercara** (Coorg) (6 hrs), **Mysore** (6 hrs).

Train Enquiries: T0497-270 5555. About 15 trains a day run north to **Mangalore** (2½ hrs) and south to **Kozhikode** (1½ hrs). Direct trains also run to **Bengaluru** (14 hrs), **Chennai** (15 hrs) via **Palakkad** (5 hrs), **Ernakulam** (6 hrs), **Madgaon** (8 hrs).

Bekal

Bekal, 16 km south of Kasaragod, has an ancient **fort** on the sea, the largest and best preserved in Kerala, which gives superb views of the coastline. Originally built by the Kadamba kings, the fort passed under the control of Vijayanagar and of Tipu Sultan before being brought into the hands of the East India Company. Excavations have exposed some interesting structures. Just outside the fort is the **Sri Mukhyaprana Temple**. North and south of the fort stretch long, largely unspoiled beaches, whose sands the Kerala tourism authorities visualize as a future Kovalam; so far there are just a couple of outlandish and isolated resorts. En route to Bekal the road passes **Ezhimala**, with a beach and a hill famous for its Ayurvedic herbs.

Kasaragod

Kasaragod is the northernmost town in Kerala. From the bus stand, the walk to the sea through a sprawling residential area – mainly Moplah – takes about 30 minutes. The beach is magnificent and deserted. You can walk a long way before scrambling back to the main road, crossing paddy fields, backwaters, and the Konkan railway line. For *Theyyam* and *Yakshagana* performances contact the **Kasaragod DTPC** (see below).

Listings Bekal and Kasaragod

Tourist information

Kasaragod DTPC
Vidya Nagar, Kasaragod, T04994-256450, www.dtpckasaragod.com.

What to do

Bekal Resorts Development Corporation, *Bekal, T0467-227 2007, www.bekal.org.* The tourism-starved north wants a piece of the houseboat action. Happily it has amazingly pristine mangroves.

The forest-shrouded shoulders of Chembra Peak stand guard over Wayanad ('land of paddy fields'), a beguiling highland district of spice farms, tea plantations, waterfalls and weird upwellings of volcanic rock, inland from Kozhikode on the picturesque road to Mysore. An easy weekend break from either city, Wayanad so far remains delightfully unspoiled, and its cool misty mornings make a refreshing contrast with the sultry coastal plains.

It's also prime wildlife spotting territory: elephants patrol the woodlands of Muthanga and Tholpetty sanctuaries, while the dense *shola* forests around Vythiri are home to whistling thrushes, leaping frogs and giant squirrels. Many of the plantation bungalows have thrown open their doors as luxurious, atmospheric homestays, and the vogue for building treehouses makes this the best place in India if you want to wake up among the branches of a fig tree looking out over virgin forest.

Kozikode to Muthanga

The road from Kozhikode to Wayanad corkscrews steeply up the Western Ghats, topping out after 65 km at **Vythiri**, a popular but low-key weekend getaway set amid stunning forests, with kayaking and nature walks available at **Pookot Lake**.

At Chundale (5 km from Vythiri) the road divides: the main route continues to busy **Kalpetta**, which offers plenty of hotels and banks but little in the way of charm, while the more appealing Ooty road leads east to **Meppadi**, the starting point for treks up wild and rugged **Chembra Peak** (2100 m) ① *Forest Range Office, Kalpetta Rd, Meppadi, T04936-282001, trekking Rs 1500 per group Plus 150 per person including guide; call ahead to check the track is open*, on whose summit lies a heart-shaped lake. Beyond Meppadi the road continues through the rolling teascapes of Ripon Estate, then through cardamom, coffee, pepper tree and vanilla plantations to reach **Vaduvanchal** (18 km).

Six kilometres south of here, **Meenmutty Falls** ① *Rs 600 per group including guide (ask for Anoop, who speaks English and knows the forest intimately)*, are Wayanad's most spectacular waterfalls, tumbling almost 300 m in three stages. An adventurous forest track leads down to a pool at the base of the second fall; take your swimming things.

Sulthan Bathery (Sultan's Battery), the main town of eastern Wayanad, was formerly known as Ganapathivattom, or 'the fields of Ganapathi'. In the 18th century Tipu Sultan built a fort here, but not much of it remains. Some 12 km southwest of the town are the **Edakkal Caves**, a natural deep crevice set high on a granite hill on which engravings

Essential Wayanad

Finding your feet

The main transport hubs are Kalpetta and Sultan Bathery, with buses from both to Kozhikode and Mysore, and from Sultan Bathery south to Ooty. Local buses connect these towns to the local transfers. However, hiring a car can save a lot of time and hassle.

dating back to the Neolithic era have been discovered. Around 30 km to the east is **Muthanga Wildlife Sanctuary** ⓘ *www.wayanad-naturetours.com/place-to-visit. php, 0700-1000 and 1500-1700 (last entry 1600), Rs 110 Indians, RS 300 foreigners, jeep entry Rs 75; jeeps can be hired for Rs 600 per safari*, part of the Nilgiri Biosphere that also includes Karnataka's Bandipur and Tamil Nadu's Mudumalai National Parks. Jeep rides in the sanctuary, noted for its elephants, leave from the entrance gate.

Listings Wayanad

Tourist information

Wayanad DTPC
North Kalpetta, T04936-202134, www.dtpcwayanad.com.
Run by the efficient and knowledgeable Dinesh, who is a good source of information on trekking and wildlife.

Where to stay

Wayanad is Kerala's treehouse capital, and has superb homestay options, but offers relatively little joy at the budget end. Cheaper places are generally restricted to Kalpetta and Sulthan Bathery.

$$$$ Vythiri Resort
6 km up dirt road east of highway, T04936-255366, www.vythiriresort.com.
Beautiful resort hidden beside a tumbling forest stream, with a choice of cute *paadi* rooms (low beds and secluded courtyards with outdoor shower), high-ceilinged cottages, or a pair of superb new treehouses in the branches of fig trees, one of which involves being hand-winched up and down. Leisure facilities include spa, pool (swimming and 8-ball), badminton and yoga, and there's a good outdoor restaurant (buffet meals included in price) where you can watch monkeys trying to make away with the leftovers.

$$$ Aranyakam
Valathur (south of Ripon off Meppadi– Vaduvanchal Rd), T04936-280261, T(0)9447-781203, www.aranyakam.com.
Atmospheric homestay in Rajesh and Nima's 70-year-old bungalow, set amid a sea of coffee bushes and avocado trees. Huge rooms in the elegant main house come with raked bare-tile ceilings and balconies, or opt for the valley-facing treehouses where you can look out for deer and sloth bear while watching sunset over Chembra Peak. Nima serves genuine home-style Kerala food in the thatched, open-sided dining room.

$$$ Edakkal Hermitage
On road before Edakkal Caves, T04936-260123, www.edakkal.com.
A sustainable tourism initiative with 5 comfortable cottages and a sweet, simple treehouse, built in, around and on top of a series of huge boulders. Tree frogs inhabit the bamboo-fringed pond, and the sunset views over paddy fields and mountain ranges are magic. The highlight, though, is dinner, served in a natural grotto that's lit with hundreds of candles. Price includes meals.

$$-$ Haritagiri
Padmaprabha Rd, T04936-203145, www.hotelharitagiri.com.
Rs 1900-3200 (plus taxes). A modern building in the heart of Kalpetta just off the highway, some a/c rooms, clean and

comfortable, restaurant 'reasonable', good value but rather noisy.

$$-$ Regency
On the main road in Sulthan Bathery, T04936-220512, www.issacsregency.com.
Good range of neat and tidy rooms, better value at the cheaper end.

$ PPS Tourist Home
Just off highway at south end of Kalpetta, T04936-203431.
Reasonable rooms, good cheap restaurant.

What to do

The Blue Yonder *see page 110*. Can arrange excellent, forest-savvy guides.

Transport

Bus From **Kalpetta Bus Stand**, T04936-203040, to **Kozhikode**, 3½ hrs, via **Vythiri**; **Mysore** via Sulthan Bathery. From **Sulthan Bathery**, T04936-220217, to **Ambalavayal** (for **Edakkal Caves**), **Vaduvanchal** and **Ooty**.

Lakshadweep

The islands which make up the Lakshadweep ('100,000 islands') group have superb beaches and beautiful lagoons to rival the Maldives, but visiting them requires time and patience, and a willingness to slum it for a few nights. There are, despite the name, only 11 inhabited and 25 uninhabited islands making up the group. Minicoy, the southernmost island, is 183 km from Kalpeni, its nearest neighbour. Geologically they are the northernmost extensions of the chain of coral islands that extends from the far south of the Maldives. The atolls are formed of belts of coral rocks almost surrounding semi-circular lagoons, with none more than 4 m above sea level. They are rich in guano, deposits of centuries of bird droppings. The wealth of coral formations (including black coral) attracts a variety of tropical fish including angel, clown, butterfly, surgeon, sweetlip, snappers and groupers. There are also manta and sting rays, harmless sharks and green and hawksbill turtles. At the right time of the year you may be able to watch turtles laying their eggs. Arriving on the beach at night, each lays 100-200 eggs in holes they make in the sand.

Essential Lakshadweep

The islands are 225-450 km west of Kerala and have a total land area of 32 sq km. The 11 inhabited islands support a population of 60,600. You can only visit the islands on a package tour. Lakshadweep Tourism's **Society for Promotion of Recreational Tourism and Sports (SPORTS)** and other tour operators organize package tours. Everyone needs a permit, for which you need to provide details of the place and date of birth, passport number, date and place of issue, expiry date and four photos; apply two months ahead. If you plan to dive, get a doctor's certificate. Foreign tourists may only visit Agatti, Kadmat, Kalpeni and the uninhabited islets of Bangaram, Thinnakara, Suheli Par and Cherium; Indians can also visit Kavaratti and Minicoy. Thinakkara and Cheriyam are being developed. For details, see What to do and Transport, page 130.

Tip...
Agatti has a medical centre; emergencies on the islands have helicopter back-up.

The islands

isolated archipelago of beautiful islands with pristine coral reefs

Kavaratti and Agatti

Kavaratti, the administrative capital, is in the centre of the archipelago. The Ajjara and Jamath mosques have the best woodcarvings and the former has a particularly good ceiling carved out of driftwood; a well nearby is believed to have medicinal water. The aquarium with tropical fish and corals, the lake nearby and the tombs are the other sights. The woodcarving in the Ajjara is by superb local craftsmen and masons. Kayaks and windsurfers are available for rent, there's a dive centre, plus a bank and a few *dhabas* selling local food.

Some of the other islands in this group are **Andratti**, one of the largest which was first to be converted to Islam, and **Agatti**, which has Lakshadweep's airport, a beautiful lagoon and a palm-shaded resort.

Bangaram, Thinnakara and Kalp

Until recently, uninhabited Bangaram was the best place to stay on the islands, but owing to a dispute with the Lakshadweep administration, the Bangaram Island Resort is closed indefinitely. It's still possible to visit and stay at the very basic SPORTS-managed tented resort.

Across the atoll from Bangaram, tiny Thinnakara has beautiful white sand, views of sunset over the water, and another small tented resort.

Kalpeni and Suheli Par

Kalpeni, with its group of three smaller uninhabited satellite islands, is surrounded by a lagoon rich in corals, which offers excellent snorkelling and diving. The raised coral banks on the southeast and eastern shores are remains of a violent storm in 1847; the Moidin Mosque to the south has walls made of coral. The islands are reputedly free from crime; the women dress in wrap-around *lungis* (sarongs), wearing heavy gold ornaments here without any fear. Villagers entertain tourists with traditional dances, *Kolkali* and *Parichakkali*, illustrating themes drawn from folk and religious legends and accompanied by music and singing.

Suheli Par, 47 km southwest of Kavaratti, consists of a pair of uninhabited islands set on a large atoll. Utterly uninhabited, the atoll forms one of the most important turtle breeding sites in Lakshadweep. The islands' administration plans to build tourist infrastructure in the near future.

Minicoy

Minicoy (Maliku), the southernmost and largest island, is interesting because of its unique Maldivian character, having become a part of the archipelago more recently. Most people speak *Mahl* (similar to *Dhivehi*; the script is written right to left) and follow many of their customs. The ancient seafaring people have been sailing long distances for centuries and the consequential dominance by women may have led Marco Polo to call this a 'female island'. Each of the nine closely knit matrilineal communities lives in an *athir* (village) and is headed by a *Moopan*. The village houses are colourfully furnished with carved wooden furniture. Tuna fishing is a major activity and the island has a cannery and ice storage. The superb lagoon of the palm-fringed crescent-shaped island is enclosed by coral reefs. Good views from the top of the 50-m lighthouse built by the British. You can stay at the **Tourist Huts**.

Amindivi Islands

The Amindivi group consists of the northern islands of **Chetlat**, **Bitra** (the smallest, heavily populated by birds, for a long time a rich source of birds' eggs), **Kiltan** where ships from Aden called en route to Colombo, **Kadmat** and the densely populated **Amini**, rich in coconut palms, which was occupied by the Portuguese. **Kadmat**, an inhabited island 9 km long and only 200 m wide, has a beach and lagoon to the east and west, ideal for swimming and diving. The **Tourist Huts** shaded by palms are away from the local village. The Water Sports Institute has experienced qualified instructors. There are 10 executive and **Tourist Cottages** and a **Youth Hostel** with a dorm for 40.

Where to stay

Kadmat and Agatti islands have basic tourist cottages resembling local huts. Each hut has 1-2 bedrooms, mosquito nets, fans and attached baths; electricity is wind or diesel. Bangaram and Thinnakara are more basic still, with no-frills tents offered at the startling price of Rs 10,000 per night. Meals are served on the beach and are similar to Keralite cuisine, with plenty of coconut. Breakfast might be iddlis or *puris* with vegetables. Lunch and dinner might be rice and vegetable curry, sambhar, meat or fish curry. Vegetarian meals available on request.

What to do

Tourism is still in its infancy and facilities on the islands are limited. Package tours (the only way to visit) are relatively expensive. Tours operate Oct-May; most are late Jan to mid-May. Schedules may change, so allow for extra days when booking onward travel. For a full list of authorized tour operators, see www.lakshadweeptourism.com/agents.html.

SPORTS (Lakshadweep Tourism), *Indira Gandhi Rd, Willingdon Island, Kochi, T0484-266 8387, T0484-266 6789*. Offers a variety of cruise- and island-based packages, starting from Rs 25,000 per person. Also handles bookings for (overpriced) tent resorts on Thinnakara and Bangaram islands.

Watersports
Activities include windsurfing, scuba diving (**Dolphin Dive Centre** on Kavaratti, **Kadmat Diving Centre** and **Diveline**, Agatti), parasailing, waterskiing and snorkelling. Deep-sea fishing (barracuda, sailfish, yellow-fin, trevally) is possible on local boats with crew; serious anglers should bring their own equipment; no diving or deep-sea fishing Apr-Sep.

Transport

Air   Agatti has a basic airport. **Indian Airlines** and **Kingfisher** fly to/from **Kochi**, daily except Tue and Sun.

Ferry   Ferries connect the islands with **Kochi**, **Mangalore** and **Beypore** (Kozhikode). The crossing takes a minimum of 14 hrs, depending on which island you're heading for. Ship anchors 30-45 mins away from each island; passengers are ferried from there.

Inter-island transfers are by helicopter (when available) during monsoons, 15 May-15 Sep (return US$60), or by pablo boats for 8.

Background

History

The Cheras, who established themselves in the Kuttanad region around Alappuzha as the first Kerala power, developed a wide network of trade links in which both the long-established Christian community and the Jewish community participated fully. However, the neighbouring Cholas launched several successful attacks against Chera power from AD 985. When Chola power disintegrated at the end of the 11th century, Calicut gradually became dominant under the Zamorin (literally 'Lord of the Sea'), who had well-established contacts with the Arab world. By some accounts the Zamorins were the wealthiest rulers in contemporary India, but were never able to use these advantages to unite Kerala, and during the 16th century the Portuguese exploited the rivalry of the Raja of Kolattiri with the Zamorin of Calicut, being granted permission to trade from Kochi in 1499. Over the following century there was fierce competition and sometimes open warfare between the Portuguese, bent on eliminating Arab trading competition, and the Zamorin, whose prosperity depended on that Arab trade. After a century of hostility, the Dutch arrived on the west coast. The Zamorin seized the opportunity of gaining external support, and on 11 November 1614 concluded a treaty giving the Dutch full trading rights. In 1615 the British East India Company was also given the right to trade by the Zamorin. By 1633 the Dutch had captured Portuguese forts. The ruler of Kochi rapidly made friends with the Dutch, in exchange for having the new Mattancherry Palace built for him. In the decade after 1740 Raja Marthanda Varma succeeded in uniting a number of petty states around Thiruvananthapuram and led them to a crushing victory over the Dutch in the Battle of Kolachel in 1741. By 1758 the Zamorin of Calicut was forced to withdraw from Kochi, but the Travancore ruler's reign was brief. In 1766 Haidar Ali had led his cavalry troops down onto the western coastal plain, and he and his son Tipu Sultan pushed further and further south with a violence that is still bitterly remembered. In 1789, as Tipu was preparing to launch a final assault on the south of Travancore, the British attacked him from the east. He withdrew his army from Kerala and the Zamorin and other Kerala leaders looked to the British to take control of the forts held by Tipu's officers. Tipu Sultan's first defeat at the hands of Lord Cornwallis led to the Treaty of Seringapatam in 1792, under which Tipu surrendered all his captured territory in northern Kerala, to direct British rule. Travancore and Kochi then became Princely states under ultimate British authority.

Modern Kerala

Government

Kerala politics have often been unstable – even turbulent – since the first elections were held in March 1957, when Kerala became the first state in the world to democratically elect a Communist government. In contrast to many other parts of India, politics in Kerala have remained mostly secular, as the Hindu BJP's failure to gain a substantial foothold suggests. The debate has always been dominated by the struggle between the Marxist branch of the Communist Party of India (CPI-M), the Congress and various minor parties; and the state government has often been formed by coalitions. Since the late 1970s these have formed around two relatively stable "fronts": the Congress-led United Democratic Front, and the CPI-M Left Democratic Front. Control of the state has passed back and forth between the two at every election since 1982, with the UDF holding power at the time of writing.

Economy

Traditionally Kerala's economy has depended heavily on agriculture. Estate crops, especially tea and rubber, make a major contribution to exports, while coconut and coconut products like coir (the coarse fibre used for matting and string and rope production), or copra (the oil-rich flesh of the coconut), continue to be vital to the state. Recent decades have seen the rise of Kerala as a remittance economy, with large flows of money being repatriated by Malayali workers in the Gulf to invest in land, housing and small-scale industries. Highly educated and increasingly middle class, Keralites have been abandoning old-fashioned and 'menial' industries such as agriculture. Rice production has been in long-term decline, as farmers converted paddy land to other more profitable uses, and where farm fields still exist, they are largely run by Tamils or other migrant workers – who in turn earn more in Kerala than in their home states. However, instability in the economy of the United Arab Emirates (which hosts 35% of Keralites working overseas) has seen a reverse exodus, with thousands of workers across all sectors returning to Kerala in recent years. The challenge this poses to the state is enormous, not only in supporting the families affected, but in managing a population whose aspirations and debts have been built around Gulf salaries. Business leaders bemoan the leftist culture of the state and the stranglehold the trade unions have on its workforce, which makes for a working week dominated by strikes, thus barring the way for the high levels of foreign investment that have driven the rapid development of Bengaluru, Hyderabad and Chennai's urban economies.

Culture

The distinctiveness of Kerala's cultural identity is reflected in the Brahmin myths of its origin. Parasurama, the sixth incarnation of Vishnu, having been banished from India, was given permission by Varuna, the Lord of the Sea, to reclaim all the land within the throw of his axe. When Parasurama threw the axe it fell from Kanniyakumari to Gokarna, and as the sea withdrew Kerala was formed.

Cuisine

Kerala's cuisine reflects its diverse religious traditions, its location on the seaboard and the ubiquitous presence of the coconut. Uniquely in India, beef is widely eaten, although seafood is far more common. Fish moilee is prepared with coconut milk and spices while for pollichathu the fish is baked with chilli paste, curry leaves and spices. Coconut-based dishes such as thoran, a dry dish of mixed vegetables chopped very small, herbs and curry leaves, and avial, similar to thoran but cooked in a sauce, are widely eaten. Erisseri is a thick curry of banana or yam and kichadi is beetroot or cucumber in coconut-curd paste. You can try these with the soft centred, lacy pancake appam or the soft noodle rice cakes iddiappam. Jack fruit, pineapples, custard apples and an endless variety of bananas also play a vital part in many dishes. For dessert, you might get milk payasam, made with rice or vermicelli.

Dance

The special dance form of Kerala, Kathakali, has its origins in the Theyyam, a ritual tribal dance of North Kerala, and Kalaripayattu, the martial arts practised by the high-caste Nayars, going back 1000 years. In its present form of dance-drama, Kathakali has evolved over the last 400 years. The performance is usually outdoors, the stage bare but for a large bronze oil lamp, with the drummers on one side and the singers with cymbal and gong, who act as narrators, on the other. The art of mime reaches its peak in these highly stylized performances which used to last through the night; now they often take just three to four hours. The costume is comprised of a large billowing skirt, a padded jacket, some heavy ornaments and headgear. The make-up is all-important: Pacha (green) characterizing the Good and Kathi (knife, shape of a painted 'moustache'), the Villain; Thadi (bearded), white for superhuman hanumans, black for the hunter and red for evil and fierce demons; Kari (black) signifying demonesses; Minukku (shining) 'simple' make-up representing the Gentle and Spiritual. The paints are natural pigments while the stiff 'mask' is created with rice paste and lime. The final application of a flower seed in the lower eyelid results in the red eyes you will see on stage. This classical dance requires lengthy, hard training to make the body supple, the eyes expressive. The 24 mudras express the nine emotions of serenity, wonder, kindness, love, valour, fear, contempt, loathing and anger. The gods and mortals play out their roles amid the chaos brought about by human ambition, but the dance ends in peace and harmony restored by the gods.

Language
Malayalam, the state language, is the most recent of the Dravidian languages, developing from the 13th century with its origin in Sanskrit.

Matriarchy
This may have originated in the 10th-century conflict with the Cholas. Krishna Chaitanya suggests that as many men were slaughtered there was a surplus of women, encouraging the development of a matrilineal system in which women controlled family property. Kerala is the first state in India to claim 100% literacy in some districts and women enjoy a high social status. The 2011 Census shows that overall literacy has reached 94%, and almost uniquely in India there are more women than men in the population.

Religion

The majority of the population is Hindu, but more than a quarter is Muslim and there is also a large Christian population, which traces its arrival in Kerala back to St Thomas the Apostle's landing at Kodungallur in AD 52. Kerala has, to date, been a model of religious harmony: Hindus and Muslims have long been involved in each others' affairs (a fact most poignantly attested by the 16th-century Jama Masjid at Ponnani, designed and built to resemble a Hindu temple by the Hindu carpenter who lies buried within its grounds), and the communities continue to rub along peacefully. As a visitor, however, be aware that most Hindu temples are strict about admitting only Hindus to their inner sanctums.

Practicalities

Getting there

India is accessible by air from virtually every continent and, thanks to excellent connections through the Gulf and Southeast Asia, it's as easy to fly straight into Kerala as to come via the usual international gateways of Mumbai and New Delhi.

There are international airports at Kochi, Kozhikode (still listed under its old name of Calicut by some airline booking systems) and Thiruvananthapuram (Trivandrum). Any one of these makes for a relatively stress-free entry to India. Several carriers permit 'open-jaw' travel, making it possible to fly into one airport and out of another – a great option if you want to explore the full length of Kerala without having to backtrack to your point of arrival.

The cheapest return flights to Kochi from London start from around £400 in the low season, but leap to £800+ as you approach the high seasons of Christmas, New Year and Easter.

From Europe
Despite the increases to Air Passenger Duty, Britain remains the cheapest place in Europe for flights to India. **British Airways**, **Virgin Atlantic**, **Jet Airways** and **Air India** all fly direct from London to Mumbai, while **British Airways** also flies direct to Chennai, Bengaluru and Hyderabad.

Air India and **Jet Airways** offer direct services to Mumbai from several airports in mainland Europe, while major European flag carriers, including **KLM** and **Lufthansa**, fly to Mumbai from their respective hub airports.

If you're heading straight to Kerala, the cheapest and most convenient flights are generally with Middle Eastern airlines, transiting via airports in the Gulf. Several airlines from the Middle East (including **Emirates**, **Etihad**, **Gulf Air**, **Kuwait Airways**, **Qatar Airways** and **Oman Air**) offer good fares from a wide choice of British and European airports to Kochi or Thiruvananthapuram via their hub cities. This may add a couple of hours to the journey time, but allows you to avoid the more fraught route via Mumbai, which involves long immigration queues and shuttling from the international to the domestic terminal. Consolidators in the UK can quote some competitive fares, such as www.skyscanner.net, www.ebookers.com, or **North South Travel** ⓘ *T01245-608291, www.northsouthtravel.co.uk (profits to charity)*.

From North America
From the east coast, several airlines including **Air India**, **Jet Airways**, **Continental** and **Delta** fly direct from New York to Mumbai, from where you can pick up an internal flight to Kerala. **American** flies from Chicago. Discounted tickets on **British Airways**, **KLM**, **Lufthansa**, **Gulf Air** and **Kuwait Airways** are sold through agents, although they will invariably fly via their country's capital city. From the west coast, your best option is to fly to Kochi (or Chennai for a greater choice of flights) via Hong Kong, Singapore or Thailand, using those countries' national carriers. **Air Canada** operates between

Vancouver and Delhi, which also has good internal connections to Kerala. **Air Brokers International** ⓘ *www.airbrokers.com*, is competitive and reputable. **STA Travel** ⓘ *www.statravel.com*, has offices in many US cities, Toronto and Ontario. Student fares are also available from **Travel Cuts** ⓘ *www.travelcuts.com*, in Canada.

From Australasia
Qantas, **Singapore Airlines**, **Thai Airways**, **Malaysian Airlines**, **Cathay Pacific** and **Air India** are the principal airlines connecting the continents, although none have direct flights to the south. **Singapore Airlines** offers the most flexibility, with subsidiary **Silk Air** flying to Kochi and Thiruvananthapuram. Low-cost carriers, including **Air Asia** (via Kuala Lumpur), **Scoot** and **Tiger Airways** (Singapore), offer flights to Kochi at substantial savings, though long layovers and possible missed connections make this a potentially more risky venture than flying with the mainstream airlines. **STA** and **Flight Centre** offer discounted tickets from their branches in major cities in Australia and New Zealand.

Airport information
The formalities on arrival in India have been increasingly streamlined during the last few years and the facilities at the major international airports greatly improved. However, arrival can still be a slow process. Disembarkation cards, with an attached customs declaration, are handed out to passengers during the inward flight. The immigration form should be handed in at the immigration counter on arrival. The customs slip will be returned, for handing over to customs officials on leaving the baggage collection hall. You may well find that there are delays of over an hour at immigration in processing passengers who need help with filling in forms. When departing, note that you'll need to have a printout of your itinerary to get into the airport, and the security guards will only let you into the terminal within three hours of your flight. Many airports require you to scan your bags before checking in and in rare cases you may also be asked to identify your checked luggage after going through immigration and security checks.

Departure charges
Many Indian airports charge a Passenger Service Fee or User Development Fee to each departing passenger. This is normally incorporated in the ticket price, but in some cases (when fees have increased or been newly introduced) you may need to pay in person before checking in. Keep some spare cash in rupees just in case.

Getting around

Air

India has a comprehensive flight network linking the major cities of the different states. Deregulation of the airline industry has had a transformative effect on travel within India, with a host of low-budget private carriers jockeying to provide the lowest prices or highest frequency on popular routes. On any given day, booking a few days in advance, you can expect to fly between Mumbai and Kochi for around US$100 one way including taxes, while booking a month in advance can reduce the price to US$60-70.

Competition from the efficiently run private sector has, in general, improved the quality of services provided by the nationalized airlines. It also seems to herald the end of the two-tier pricing structure, meaning that ticket prices are now usually the same for foreign and Indian travellers. The airport authorities, too, have made efforts to improve handling on the ground.

Although it is comparatively expensive and delays and re-routing can be irritating, flying is an option worth considering for covering vast distances or awkward links on a route. For short distances (eg Thiruvananthapuram–Kochi), and on routes where you can sleep during an overnight journey it makes more sense to travel by train.

The best way to get an idea of the current routes, carriers and fares is to use a third-party booking website such as www.cheapairticketsindia.com (toll-free numbers: UK T0800-101 0928, USA T1-888 825 8680), www.cleartrip.com, www.makemytrip.co.in, or www.yatra.com. Booking with these is a different matter: some refuse foreign credit cards outright, while others have to be persuaded to give your card special clearance. Tickets booked on these sites are typically issued as an email ticket or an SMS text message – the simplest option if you have an Indian mobile phone, though it must be converted to a paper ticket at the relevant carrier's airport offices before you will be allowed into the terminal. Makemytrip.com and Travelocity.com both accept international credit cards.

Online train bookings from outside India

If your time is short and you plan to do a lot of train travel on popular routes with limited services (eg Kerala–Goa–Mumbai) it can be worth trying to reserve your tickets before arriving in India. Be warned, though: online booking is a dazzlingly frustrating process, because IRCTC, the Indian Railways portal that handles all ticket bookings, does not accept foreign credit cards. Nevertheless, with a degree of perseverance it can be done.

You first need to open an account with www.cleartrip.com and begin a dummy train booking, from which point you can register as a user of IRCTC. In this process you'll need to submit an Indian mobile number and postal code – make up any 10-digit number for the former and any six-digit number for the latter.

You should receive an email from IRCTC containing a one-time password (OTP). You'll then need to email care@irctc.co.in, quoting your IRCTC username and attaching a copy of your passport (under 1MB in size), and ask them to email you the separate and all-important SMS OTP. (This may take up to a week, and several chase-up emails.) Once you've got both passwords, you can activate your link with Cleartrip, and, if all goes smoothly, begin booking trains.

This process changes often, so before starting it's worth consulting the very active India transport forums at www.indiamike.com.

Rail

India's rail network is a thing of wonder, and train travel in the country is an astonishing bargain: you can spend three nights travelling the length of India by air-conditioned sleeper for slightly less than the cost of a London–Birmingham day return. As well as being the cheapest and most comfortable means of travelling long distances, a train ticket gives you access to railway station Retiring Rooms, basic but usually clean digs within the station which can be a cheap and convenient option for late arrivals or early departures. Above all, you have an ideal opportunity to meet local travellers and catch a glimpse of life on the ground.

High-speed trains

There are several air-conditioned 'high-speed' **Shatabdi** (or 'Century') **Express** for day travel, and **Rajdhani Express** ('Capital City') for overnight journeys. These cover large sections of the network but due to high demand you need to book them well in advance (up to 90 days). Meals and drinks are usually included.

Buying tickets

It's best to book your train tickets as far in advance as possible (currently up to 120 days), as trains on popular routes – and all trains during holiday periods – fill up well ahead of departure.

You can reserve tickets for virtually any train on the network from one of the 3000-plus computerized reservation centres across India. To reserve a seat at a booking office, note down the train's name, number and departure time and fill in a reservation form before you line up at the ticket window; you can use one form for up to four passengers. At busy stations the wait can take an hour or more.

You can save a lot of time and effort by asking a travel agent to get your tickets for a fee of Rs 50-100. If the class you want is full, ask if tickets are available under any of Indian Rail's special quotas. **Foreign Tourist Quota** (**FTQ**) reserves a small number of tickets on popular routes for overseas travellers; you need your passport and either an exchange certificate or ATM receipt to book tickets under FTQ. The other useful special quota is **Tatkal**, which releases a last-minute pool of tickets on the day before the train departs (at 1000 for a/c classes and 1100 for non-a/c). If the quota system can't help you, consider buying a 'wait list' ticket, as seats often become available close to the train's departure time; you can check your wait list status at www.indiarailinfo.com, or phone the station on the day of departure to check your ticket's status. If you don't have a reservation for a particular train but carry an **Indrail Pass**, you may get one by arriving three hours early. **Note** Be wary of touts at the station offering tickets, hotels or exchange.

Classes
A/c First Class, available only on main routes, is the choice of the Indian upper crust, with two- or four-berth carpeted sleeper compartments with washbasin. As with all a/c sleeper accommodation, bedding is included, and the windows are tinted to the point of being almost impossible to see through. **A/c Sleeper**, two- and three-tier configurations (known as 2AC and 3AC), are clean and comfortable and popular with middle-class families; these are the safest carriages for women travelling alone. **A/c Executive Class**, with wide reclining seats, are available on many Shatabdi trains at double the price of the ordinary **a/c Chair Car** which are equally comfortable. **First Class (non-a/c)** is gradually being phased out, and is now restricted to a handful of routes through Tamil Nadu and Kerala, but the run-down old carriages still provide a very enjoyable combination of privacy and windows you can open. **Second Class (non-a/c)** two- and three-tier (commonly called **Sleeper**) provides exceptionally cheap and atmospheric travel, with basic padded vinyl seats and open windows that allow the sights and sounds of India (not to mention dust, insects and flecks of spittle expelled by passengers up front) to drift into the carriage. On long journeys Sleeper can be crowded and uncomfortable, and toilet facilities can be unpleasant; it is nearly always better to use the Indian-style squat loos rather than the Western-style ones as they are better maintained. At the bottom rung is **Unreserved Second Class**, with hard wooden benches. You can travel long distances for a trivial amount of money, but unreserved carriages are often ridiculously crowded, and getting off at your station may involve a battle of will and strength against the hordes trying to shove their way on.

Indrail passes
These allow travel across the entire Indian railway network, but you have to spend a high proportion of your time on the train to make it worthwhile. However, the advantages of pre-arranged reservations and automatic access to 'Tourist Quotas' can tip the balance in favour of the pass for some travellers.

Tourists (foreigners and Indians resident abroad) may buy these passes from the tourist sections of principal railway booking offices and pay in foreign currency, major credit cards, traveller's cheques or rupees with encashment certificates. Fares range from US$57 to US$1060 for adults or half that for children.

Indrail passes can also conveniently be bought abroad from special agents. For people contemplating a single long journey soon after arriving in India, the half- or one-day pass with a confirmed reservation is worth the peace of mind; two- or four-day passes are also sold.

The UK agent is **SDEL** ⓘ *103 Wembley Park Dr, Wembley, Middlesex HA9 8HG, UK, T020-8903 3411, www.indiarail.co.uk*, which makes all necessary reservations and offers excellent advice. They can also advise on **Jet Airways** and other internal flights.

Railpass prices

Period	US$ A/c 2-tier	Period	US$ A/c 2-tier
½ day	26	21 days	198
1 day	43	30 days	248
7 days	135	60 days	400
15 days	185	90 days	530

Cost

Fares for individual journeys are based on distance covered and reflect both the class and the type of train. Higher rates apply on the Mail and Express trains and the air-conditioned Shatabdi and Rajdhani expresses.

A/c First Class costs about double the rate for two-tier shown above, and non a/c Sleeper class about half. Children (aged five to 12) travel at half the adult fare. The young (12-30 years) and senior citizens (65 years and over) are allowed a 30% discount on journeys over 500 km (just show your passport).

Rail travel tips

Bedding It can get cold in air-conditioned coaches when travelling at night. Bedding is provided on second class air-conditioned sleepers. On others it can be hired for Rs 30 from the Station Baggage Office for second class.

Berths It is worth asking for upper berths, especially in second class three-tier sleepers, as they can also be used during the day when the lower berths are used as seats. Once the middle berth is lowered for sleeping the lower berth becomes too cramped to sit on. Passengers with valid tickets but no berth reservations are sometimes permitted to travel overnight, causing great discomfort to travellers occupying lower berths.

Delays Delays are common on all types of transport, and it's vital to allow plenty of time for making connections. The special **Shatabdi** and **Rajdhani Express** are generally quite reliable. Ordinary Express and Mail trains have priority over local services and occasionally surprise by being punctual, but generally the longer the journey time, the greater the delay. Delays on the rail network are cumulative, so arrivals and departures from mid-stations are often several hours behind schedule. Allow at least two hours for connections, more if the first part of the journey is long distance.

TRAVEL TIP

Train touts

Many railway stations – and some bus stations and major tourist sites – are heavily populated with touts. Self-styled 'agents' will board trains before they enter the station and seek out tourists, often picking up their luggage and setting off with words such as "Madam!/Sir! Come with me madam/sir! You need top-class hotel …". They will even select porters to take your luggage without giving you any say.

If you have succeeded in getting off the train or even in obtaining a trolley you will find hands eager to push it for you.

For a first-time visitor such touts can be more than a nuisance. You need to keep calm and firm. Decide in advance where you want to stay. If you need a porter on trains, select one yourself and agree a price **before** the porter sets off with your baggage. If travelling with a companion one can stay guarding the luggage while the other finds a taxi and negotiates the price to the hotel. It sounds complicated and sometimes it feels it. The most important thing is to behave as if you know what you are doing!

Food and drink It is best to carry some, though tea, bottled water and snacks are sold on trains and platforms. Carry plenty of small notes and coins on long journeys. On long-distance trains, the restaurant car is often near the upper-class carriages.

Internet services Much information is available online via www.railtourism india.com, www.indianrail.gov.in, www.erail.in and the brilliantly useful www.india railinfo.com, where you can check timetables (which change frequently), train numbers, seat availability, the running status of your train, and even forums discussing the cleanliness, average delay, and food quality of each individual train on the network.

Ladies' compartments A woman travelling alone, overnight, on an unreserved second-class train can ask if there is one of these. Lone female travellers may feel more comfortable in air-conditioned sleeper coaches, which require reservations and are used by Indian families.

Ladies' and seniors' queues Separate (much shorter) ticket queues may be available for women and senior citizens. Travellers over 60 can ask for a 30% discount on the ticket price.

Left luggage Bags can be left for up to 30 days in station cloakrooms. These are especially useful when there is time to go sightseeing before an evening train. The bags must be lockable and you are advised not to leave any food in them.

Overbooking Passengers with valid tickets but no berth reservations are sometimes permitted to travel overnight, causing great discomfort to travellers occupying lower berths. Wait-listed passengers should confirm the status of their ticket in advance by calling enquiries at the nearest computerised reservation office. If you have access to www.irctc.in you can also check the waitlist status of your ticket using the PNR number or a travel agent can do this online. At the station, check the reservation charts (usually on the relevant platform) and contact the Station Manager or Ticket Collector.

Porters These can carry prodigious amounts of luggage. Rates vary from station to station (sometimes listed on a board on the platform) but are usually around Rs 10-25 per item of luggage. Establish the rate first.

Pre-paid taxis Many main stations have a pre-paid taxi (or auto-rickshaw) service which offers a reliable service at a fair price. If there are no pre-paid taxis ask your hotel for a guide price.

Security Keep valuables close to you, securely locked, and away from windows. For security, carry a good lock and chain to attach your luggage.

Timetables

Regional timetables are available cheaply from station bookstalls; the monthly *Indian Bradshaw* is sold in principal stations. The handy *Trains at a Glance* (Rs 40) lists popular trains likely to be used by most foreign travellers and is available at stalls at Indian railway stations and in the UK from SDEL (see page 144).

Road

Road travel is often the only choice for reaching many of the places of outstanding interest in which India is so rich. For the uninitiated, travel by road can also be a worrying experience because of the apparent absence of conventional traffic regulations and also in the mountains, especially during the rainy season when landslides are possible. Vehicles drive on the left – in theory. Routes around the major cities are usually crowded with lorry traffic, especially at night, and the main roads are often poor and slow. There are a few motorway-style expressways, but most main roads are single track. Some district roads are quiet, and although they are not fast they can be a good way of seeing the country and village life if you have the time.

Bus

Buses now reach virtually every part of India, offering a cheap, if often uncomfortable, means of visiting places off the rail network. Very few villages are now more than 2-3 km from a bus stop. Most services in Kerala are operated by the government-run **Kerala State Road Transport Corporation (KSRTC)** ⓘ *www.keralartc.com*. These buses depart from the central bus stand in every town. Larger towns and popular tourist destinations are also served by private bus operators, whose offices cluster around the main bus stand. The latter allow advance reservations, including booking printable e-tickets online (check www.redbus.in and www.viaworld.in) and, although tickets prices are a little higher, they have fewer stops and are a bit more comfortable. In the absence of trains, buses are often the only budget option. There are also many sleeper buses (a contradiction in terms); if you must take a sleeper bus, choose a lower berth near the front of the bus. The upper berths are almost always really uncomfortable.

Bus categories Though comfortable for sightseeing trips, apart from the very best 'sleeper coaches' even **air-conditioned luxury coaches** can be very uncomfortable for really long journeys. Often the air conditioning is very cold so wrap up. Journeys over 10 hours can be extremely tiring so it is better to go by train if there is a choice.

Express buses run over long distances (frequently overnight), these are often called 'video coaches' and can be an appalling experience unless you appreciate loud film music blasting through the night. Ear plugs and eye masks may ease the pain. They rarely average more than 45 kph. **Local buses** are often very crowded, quite bumpy, slow and usually poorly maintained. However, over short distances, they can be a very cheap, friendly and easy way of getting about. Even where signboards are not in English someone will usually give you directions. Many larger towns have **minibus** services which charge a little more than the buses and pick up and drop passengers on request. Again very crowded, and with restricted headroom, they are the fastest way of getting about many of the larger towns.

Bus travel tips Some towns have different bus stations for different destinations. Booking on major long-distance routes is now computerized. Book in advance where possible and avoid the back of the bus where it can be very bumpy. If your destination is only served by a local bus you may do better to take the Express bus and 'persuade' the driver, with a tip in advance, to stop where you want to get off. You will have to pay the full fare to the first stop beyond your destination but you will get there faster and more comfortably. When an unreserved bus pulls into a bus station, there is usually an unholy scramble for seats, whilst those arriving have to struggle to get off! In many areas there is an unwritten 'rule of reservation' using handkerchiefs or bags thrust through the windows to reserve seats. Some visitors may feel a more justified right to a seat having fought their way through the crowd, but it is generally best to do as local people do and be prepared with a handkerchief or 'sarong'. As soon as it touches the seat, it is yours! Leave it on your seat when getting off to use the toilet at bus stations.

Car

A car provides a chance to travel off the beaten track, and gives unrivalled opportunities for seeing something of India's great variety of villages and small towns. Until recently, the most widely used hire car was the romantic but notoriously unreliable Hindustan Ambassador. You can still find them for hire in parts of Kerala, but they're gradually giving way to more efficient (and boring) Tata and Toyota models with mod cons such as optional air-conditioning ... and seat belts. A handful of international agencies offer self-drive car hire (**Avis, Sixt**), but India's majestically anarchic traffic culture is not for the faint-hearted, and emphatically not a place for those who value such quaint concepts as lane discipline, or indeed driving on your assigned side of the road. It's much more common, and comfortable, to hire not just the car but someone to drive it for you.

Car hire If you fancy the idea of being Lady Penelope and gadding about with your own chauffeur, dream no more. Hiring a car and driver is the most comfortable and efficient way to cover short to medium distances, and although prices have increased sharply in recent years car travel in India is still a bargain by western standards. Even if you're travelling on a modest budget a day's car hire can help take the sting out of an arduous journey, allowing you to go sightseeing along the way without looking for somewhere to stash your bags.

Local drivers often know their way around an area much better than drivers from other states, so where possible it is a good idea to get a local driver who speaks the state language, in addition to being able to communicate with you. The best way to guarantee a driver who speaks good English is to book in advance with a professional travel agency, either in India or in your home country. Recommended operators with English speaking drivers include **Milesworth Travel** ⓘ *www.milesworth.com*, and **Intersight** ⓘ *www.intersighttours.com*. You can, if you choose, arrange car hire informally by asking around at taxi stands, but don't expect your driver to speak anything more than rudimentary English.

On pre-arranged overnight trips the fee you pay will normally include fuel and inter-state taxes – check before you pay – and a wage for the driver. Drivers are responsible for their expenses, including meals (and the pervasive servant-master culture in India means that most will choose to sit separately from you at meal times). Some tourist hotels provide rooms for drivers, but they often choose to sleep in the car overnight to save money. In some areas drivers also seek to increase their earnings by taking you to hotels and shops where they earn a handsome commission; these are generally hugely overpriced and poor alternatives to the hotels recommended in this book, so don't be afraid to say no and insist on your choice of accommodation. If you feel inclined, a tip at the end of the tour of Rs 100 per day is perfectly acceptable.

	Tata Indica non-a/c	Tata Indigo non-a/c	Hyundai Accent a/c	Toyota Innova
8 hrs/80 km	Rs 1200	Rs 1600	Rs 2200	Rs 2500
Extra km	Rs 8	Rs 10	Rs 15	Rs 15
Extra hour	Rs 80	Rs 100	Rs 200	Rs 180
Out of town				
Per km	Rs 8	Rs 10	Rs 15	Rs 15
Night halt	Rs 200	Rs 200	Rs 300	Rs 250

Taxi

Taxi travel in India is a great bargain, and in most cities in Kerala you can take a taxi from the airport to the centre for under US$15.

Yellow-top taxis in cities and large towns are metered, although tariffs change frequently. The latest rates are typically shown on a fare conversion chart which should be read in conjunction with the meter reading. Increased night time rates apply in most cities, and there might be a small charge for luggage.

Insist on the taxi meter being flagged in your presence. If the driver refuses, the official advice is to contact the police. When a taxi doesn't have a meter, you will need to fix the fare before starting the journey; ask at your hotel desk for a rough price. As a foreigner, it is rare to get a taxi in the big cities to use the meter – if they are eager to, watch out as sometimes the meter is rigged and they have a fake rate card. Also, watch out for the David Blaine-style note shuffle: you pay with a Rs 500 note, but they have a Rs 100 note in their hand.

Most airports and many major stations have booths where you can book a prepaid taxi. For slightly more than the metered fare these allow you to sidestep overcharging and give you the security of knowing that your driver will take you to your destination by the most direct route. You might be able to join up with other travellers at the booth to share a taxi to your hotel or a central point. It's OK to give the driver a small tip at the end of the journey.

At night, always have a clear idea of where you want to go and insist on being taken there. Taxi drivers may try to convince you that the hotel you have chosen 'closed three years ago' or is 'completely full'. Say that you have a reservation.

Rickshaw Auto-rickshaws (autos) are almost universally available in towns across Kerala and are the cheapest and most convenient way of getting about. It is best to walk a short distance away from a hotel gate before picking up an auto to avoid paying an inflated rate. In addition to using them for short journeys it is often possible to hire them by the hour, or for a half or full day's sightseeing. In some areas younger drivers who speak some English and know their local area well may want to show you around. However, rickshaw drivers are often paid a commission by hotels, restaurants and gift shops so advice is not always impartial. Drivers generally refuse to use a meter, often quote a ridiculous price or may sometimes stop short of your destination. If you have real problems it can help to note down the vehicle licence number and threaten to go to the police.

Cycle-rickshaws are more common in the more rustic setting of a small town or the outskirts of a large one. You will need to fix a price by bargaining.

Essentials A-Z

Accident and emergency

Contact the relevant emergency service (police T100, fire T101, ambulance T102) and your embassy. Make sure you obtain police/medical reports required for insurance claims.

Children

Children of all ages are widely welcomed. However, care should be taken when travelling to remote areas where health services are primitive. It's best to visit in the cooler months since you need to protect children from the sun, heat, dehydration and mosquito bites. Cool showers or baths help; avoid being out during the hottest part of the day. Diarrhoea and vomiting are the most common problems, so take the usual precautions. Breastfeeding is best and most convenient for babies. In the big cities you can get safe baby foods and formula milk. Wet wipes and disposable nappies are difficult to find. The biggest hotels provide babysitting. See also Health, page 151.

Customs and duty free

Duty free

Tourists are allowed to bring in all personal effects 'which may reasonably be required', without charge. The official customs allowance includes 200 cigarettes or 50 cigars, 0.95 litres of alcohol, a camera and a pair of binoculars. Valuable personal effects and professional equipment including jewellery, special camera equipment and lenses, laptop computers and sound and video recorders must in theory be declared on a Tourist Baggage Re-Export Form (TBRE) in order for them to be taken out of the country; in practice it's relatively unlikely that your bags will be inspected beyond a cursory X-ray. Nevertheless, it saves considerable frustration if you know the equipment serial numbers in advance and are ready to show them on the equipment. In addition to the forms, details of imported equipment may be entered into your passport. Save time by completing the formalities while waiting for your baggage. It is essential to keep these forms for showing to the customs when leaving India, otherwise considerable delays are very likely at the time of departure.

Currency regulations

There are no restrictions on the amount of foreign currency or TCs a tourist may bring into India. If you are carrying more than US$5000 in cash or US$10,000 or its equivalent in cash and TCs you need to fill in a currency declaration form. This could change with a relaxation in the currency regulations.

Prohibited items

The import of live plants, gold coins, gold and silver bullion and silver coins not in current use are either banned or subject to strict regulation. Enquire at consular offices abroad for details. For export restrictions see Shopping tips, page 16.

Disabled travellers

India is not geared up for the disabled or wheelchair-bound traveller. Access to buildings, toilets (sometimes squat), pavements, kerbs and public transport can prove frustrating, but it is easy to find people to give a hand to help with lifting and carrying. Provided you are prepared to pay for at least mid-priced accommodation, car hire and taxis, a visit to Kerala should be rewarding.

Some travel companies specialize in exciting holidays, tailor-made for individuals depending on their level of ability. **Global Access**, Disabled Travel Network, www.globalaccessnews.com, is dedicated to providing travel information for 'disabled adventurers' and includes a number of reviews and tips from members of the public.
Accessible Journeys Inc, 35 West Sellers Av, Ridley Park, PA 19078, T610-521 0339, www.disabilitytravel.com, runs some packages to India.
Journeys Without Barriers, www.travelanotherindia.com, is an Indian company offering a limited range of wheelchair-accessible journeys.
ResponsibleTravel.com, T01273-823700, www.responsibletravel.com, specializes in eco-friendly holidays and has some tailored to the needs of disabled travellers.

Drugs

Certain areas, such as Kovalam and Varkala, have become associated with foreigners who take drugs. These are likely to attract local and foreign drug dealers but be aware that the government takes the misuse of drugs very seriously. Anyone charged with the illegal possession of drugs risks facing a fine of Rs 100,000 and a minimum 10 years' imprisonment. Several foreigners have been imprisoned for drugs-related offences in the last decade.

Electricity

India supply is 220-240 volts AC. Some top hotels have transformers. There may be pronounced variations in the voltage, and power cuts are common. Power back-up by generator or inverter is becoming more widespread, even in humble hotels, though it may not cover a/c. Socket sizes vary so take a universal adaptor; low-quality versions are available locally. Many hotels, even in the higher categories, don't have electric razor sockets. Invest in a stabilizer for a laptop.

Embassies and consulates

For information on visas and immigration, see page 160. For a comprehensive list of embassies (but not all consulates), see http://mea.gov.in/indian-missions-abroad.htm.

Health

Local populations in India are exposed to a range of health risks not encountered in the Western world. Many of the diseases are major problems for the local poor and destitute and, although the risk to travellers is more remote, they cannot be ignored. Obviously 5-star travel is going to carry less risk than backpacking on a budget.

Health care in the region is varied. There are many excellent private and government clinics/hospitals. As with all medical care, first impressions count. It's worth contacting your embassy or consulate on arrival and asking where the recommended (ie those used by diplomats) clinics are. You can also ask about locally recommended medical do's and don'ts. If you do get ill, and you have the opportunity, you should also ask your medical insurer whether they are satisfied that the medical centre/hospital you have been referred to is of a suitable standard.

Before you go

Ideally, you should see your GP or travel clinic at least 6 weeks before your departure for general advice on travel risks, malaria and vaccinations. Make sure you have travel insurance, get a dental check (especially if you are going to be away for more than a month), know your own blood group and if you suffer a long-term condition such as diabetes or epilepsy make sure someone knows or that you have a Medic Alert bracelet/necklace with this information on it. Remember that it is risky to buy medicinal tablets abroad because the doses may differ and India has a huge trade in counterfeit drugs.

Vaccinations

If you need vaccinations, see your doctor well in advance of your travel. Most courses must be completed by a minimum of 4 weeks before you go. Travel clinics may provide rapid courses of vaccination, but are likely to be more expensive. The following vaccinations are recommended: typhoid, polio, tetanus, infectious hepatitis and diptheria. For details of malaria prevention, contact your GP or local travel clinic.

The following vaccinations may also be considered: rabies, possibly BCG (since TB is still common in the region) and in some cases meningitis and diphtheria (if you're staying in the country for a long time). Yellow fever is not required in India but you may be asked to show a certificate if you have travelled from Africa or South America. Japanese encephalitis may be required for rural travel at certain times of the year (mainly rainy seasons). An effective oral cholera vaccine (Dukoral) is now available as 2 doses providing 3 months' protection.

If you get ill

Contact your embassy or consulate for a list of doctors and dentists who speak your language, or at least some English. Good-quality healthcare is available in the larger centres but it can be expensive, especially hospitalization; see the list below. Make sure you have adequate insurance.

Alappuzha (Alleppey) and around
District Hospital, T0477-225 3324.

Fort Kochi and Ernakulam
General Hospital, Hospital Rd, Ernakulam, T0484-238 1768. **Govt Hospital**, Fort Kochi, T0484-222 4444. On MG Rd: **City**, T0484-236 1809, and **Medical Trust Hospital**, T0484-235 8001, have 24-hr pharmacies. **City Dental Clinic**, T0484-236 8164.

Kol lam (Quilon)
District Hospital, T0474-279 3409.

Kottayam and Kumarakom
District Hospital, T0481-256 3651.

Kovalam and nearby resorts
Emergency assistance either through your hotel or from **Government Hospital** in Thiruvananthapuram.
Upasana Hospital, near Le Meridien gate, T0471-248 0632, has an experienced English-speaking doctor.

Kozhikode (Calicut)
Government Hospital, T0495-236 5367. Medical. **College Hospital**, T0495-235 6531.

Munnar
Tata General Hospital, T04865-230270, on the north edge of town on the Rajamalai Rd. Excellent.

Thekkady
Kumily Central Hospital, open 0900-
1300 and 1630-2000, 24-hr call out
for emergencies.

Thiruvananthapuram
Many chemists, near hospitals; a few near
Statue Junction.
Cosmopolitan Hospital, Kumarapuram,
T0471-244 8182.
General Hospital, Vanchiyoor,
T0471-230 7874.
Ramakrishna Ashrama Hospital,
Sasthamangalam, T0471-272 2125.
Vrindavan Ayurvedic Health Centre,
Kumarapuram, T0471-244 0376.

Thrissur (Trichur)
Amala Cancer Hospital, Amalanagar
(9 km, along the Guruvayur Rd), T0487-221
1950. Recommended for medicine, surgery.

Websites
**British Travel Health Association
(UK), www.btha.org** This is the official
website of an organization of travel
health professionals.
**Fit for Travel, www.fitfortravel.scot.
nhs.uk** This site from Scotland provides
a quick A-Z of vaccine and travel health
advice requirements for each country.
**Foreign and Commonwealth Office
(FCO) (UK), www.fco.gov.uk** This is a key
travel advice site, with useful information
on the country, people, climate and lists
the UK embassies/consulates. The site also
promotes the concept of 'know before
you go' and encourages travel insurance
and appropriate travel health advice. It
has links to Department of Health travel
advice site.
**The Health Protection Agency, www.
hpa.org.uk** Up-to-date malaria advice
guidelines for travel around the world.
It gives specific advice about the right

drugs for each location. It also has useful
information for those who are pregnant,
suffering from epilepsy or planning to
travel with children.
**Medic Alert (UK), www.medicalalert.
com** This is the website of the foundation
that produces bracelets and necklaces for
those with existing medical problems.
Once you have ordered your bracelet/
necklace you write your key medical
details on paper inside it, so that if you
collapse, a medic can identify you as
having epilepsy or a nut allergy, etc.
**Travel Screening Services (UK),
www.travelscreening.co.uk** A private
clinic dedicated to integrated travel
health. The clinic gives vaccine, travel
health advice, email and SMS text vaccine
reminders and screens returned travellers
for tropical diseases.
**World Health Organisation, www.who.
int** The WHO site has links to the *WHO
Blue Book* on travel advice. This lists the
diseases in different regions of the world.
It describes vaccination schedules and
makes clear which countries have yellow
fever vaccination certificate requirements
and malarial risk.

Insurance

Insurance is strongly recommended and
policies are fairly reasonable. If you have
financial restraints, the most important
aspect of any insurance policy is medical
care and repatriation. Ideally you want to
make sure you are covered for personal
items too. Read the small print before
heading off so you are aware of what is
covered and what is not, what is required
to submit a claim and what to do in the
event of an emergency. Always buy
insurance before setting out as your
options will be more limited and generally
quite costly once you've departed from
your home country.

Language

See Language section on page 161 for useful words and phrases.

The state language of Kerala is Malayalam, an offshoot of the Dravidian family of South Indian languages. As elsewhere in South India, Hindi – the official national language – is little known here and, given the notorious difficulty of learning Malayalam, English acts as the lingua franca between locals and visitors. It is widely spoken in towns and cities and even in quite remote villages it is usually not difficult to find someone who speaks at least a little English. Outside of major tourist sites, other European languages are almost completely unknown. The accent in which English is spoken is often affected strongly by the mother tongue of the speaker and there have been changes in common grammar which sometimes make it sound unusual. Many of these changes have become standard Indian English usage, as valid as any other varieties of English used around the world.

Money

US$1= Rs 66.08, €1=Rs 70.98, £1= Rs 99.37 (Nov 2015).

Indian currency is the Indian Rupee (Re/ Rs). It is not possible to purchase these before you arrive. If you want cash on arrival it is best to get it at the airport bank, although see if an ATM is available as airport rates are not very generous. Rupee notes are printed in denominations of Rs 1000, 500, 100, 50, 20, 10. The rupee is divided into 100 paise. Coins are minted in denominations of Rs 5, Rs 2, Rs 1 and 50 paise. **Note** Carry money in a money belt worn under clothing. Have a small amount in an easily accessible place.

Credit cards

Major credit cards are increasingly acceptable in the main centres, though in smaller cities and towns it is still rare to be able to pay by credit card. Payment by credit card can sometimes be more expensive than payment by cash, whilst some credit card companies charge a premium on cash withdrawals. **Visa** and **MasterCard** have a growing number of ATMs in major cities and several banks offer withdrawal facilities for Cirrus and Maestro cardholders. It is however easy to obtain a cash advance against a credit card. Railway reservation centres in major cities take payment for train tickets by Visa card which can be very quick as the queue is short, although they cannot be used for Tourist Quota tickets.

Currency cards

If you don't want to carry lots of cash, pre-paid currency cards allow you to preload money from your bank account, fixed at the day's exchange rate. They look like a credit or debit card and are issued by specialist money changing companies, such as **Travelex** and **Caxton FX**, as well as the **Post Office**. You can top up and check your balance by phone, online and sometimes by text.

Traveller's cheques (TCs)

TCs are almost obsolete, shops and restaurants won't change them, but they do provide peace of mind against theft. Denominations of US$50 and US$100 are preferable, with a few of US$20 to increase your options. American Express or Visa US dollar TCs are recommended. Several banks charge a high fixed commission for changing TCs because they don't really want the bother. Some establishments may ask to see a passport and the customer's record of purchase before accepting. Keep the original purchase slip in a separate place to the TCs and make a photocopy for security. The better hotels will normally change TCs for their guests (often at a poor rate).

ATMs

By far the most convenient method of accessing money, ATMs are all over India, usually attended by security guards, with most banks offering some services to holders of overseas cards. Banks whose ATMs will issue cash against Cirrus and Maestro cards, as well as Visa and MasterCard, include **Bank of Baroda**, **Citibank**, **HDFC**, **HSBC**, **ICICI**, **IDBI**, **Punjab National Bank**, **State Bank of India** (**SBI**), **Standard Chartered** and **UTI**. A withdrawal fee is usually charged by the issuing bank on top of the conversion charges applied by your own bank. Fraud prevention measures quite often result in travellers having their cards blocked by the bank when unexpected overseas transactions occur; advise your bank of your travel plans before leaving.

Changing money

The **State Bank of India** and several others in major towns are authorized to deal in foreign exchange. Some give cash against Visa/MasterCard (eg **ANZ**, **Bank of Baroda** who print a list of their participating branches, **Andhra Bank**). American Express cardholders can use their cards to get either cash or TCs in Mumbai and Chennai. They also have offices in Coimbatore, Goa, Hyderabad, and Thiruvananthapuram. The larger cities have licensed money changers with offices usually in the commercial sector. Changing money through unauthorized dealers is illegal. Premiums on the currency black market are very small and highly risky. Large hotels change

money 24 hrs a day for guests, but banks often give a substantially better rate of exchange. It is best to exchange money on arrival at the airport bank or the **Thomas Cook** counter. Many international flights arrive during the night and it is generally far easier and less time consuming to change money at the airport than in the city. You should be given a foreign currency encashment certificate when you change money through a bank or authorized dealer; ask for one if it is not automatically given. It allows you to change Indian rupees back to your own currency on departure. It also enables you to use rupees to pay hotel bills or buy air tickets for which payment in foreign exchange may be required. The certificates are only valid for 3 months.

Cost of travelling

Most food, accommodation and public transport, especially rail and bus, is exceptionally cheap, although inflation is pushing prices up at a drastic rate and the cost of basic food items such as rice, lentils, tomatoes and onions have skyrocketed. There is a widening range of moderately priced but clean hotels and restaurants outside the big cities, making it possible to get a great deal for your money.

Budget travellers sharing a room, taking public transport, avoiding souvenir stalls, and eating nothing but rice and dhal can get away with a budget of Rs 600-800 (about US$9-12 or £6-8) a day. This sum leaps up if you drink alcohol (still cheap by European standards at about US$2, £1 or Rs 80 for a pint), smoke foreign-brand cigarettes or want to have your own wheels (you can expect to spend between Rs 250 and Rs 500 to hire a scooter per day). Those planning to stay in fairly comfortable hotels and use taxis sightseeing should budget at

US$50-80 (£30-50) a day. Then again you could always check into the **Taj** in Kumarakom for Christmas and notch up an impressive US$600 (£350) bill on your B&B alone. India can be a great place to pick and choose, save a little on basic accommodation and then treat yourself to the type of meal you could only dream of affording back home. Also, be prepared to spend a fair amount more in Fort Kochi and the Backwaters, where not only is the cost of living significantly higher but where it's worth coughing up extra for a half-decent room: penny-pinch by the beach when you'll be spending precious little time indoors anyway. A newspaper costs Rs 5-10 and breakfast for 2 with coffee can come to as little as Rs 150 in a South Indian 'hotel', but if you intend to eat banana pancakes or pasta by the beach in Varkala, you can expect to pay more like Rs 200-400 a plate.

Opening hours

Banks Mon-Fri 1030-1430, Sat 1030-1230. Top hotels sometimes have a 24-hr money changing service. **Post offices** Mon-Fri 1000-1700, often shutting for lunch, and Sat mornings. **Government offices** Mon-Fri 0930-1700, Sat 0930-1300 (some open on alternate Sat only). **Shops** Mon-Sat 0930-1800. Bazars keep longer hours.

Safety

Personal security

In general the threats to personal security for travellers in India are remarkably small. However, incidents of petty theft and violence directed specifically at tourists have been on the increase so care is necessary in some places, and basic common sense needs to be used with respect to looking after valuables. Follow the same precautions you would when at home. There have been incidents of sexual assault in and around the main tourist beach centres, particularly after full moon parties in South India. Avoid wandering alone outdoors late at night in these places. During daylight hours be careful in remote places, especially when alone. If you are under threat, scream loudly. Be very cautious before accepting food or drink from casual acquaintances, as it may be drugged – though note that Indians on a long train journey will invariably try to share their snacks with you, and balance caution with the opportunity to interact.

Unaccompanied women are most vulnerable in major cities, crowded bazars, beach resorts and tourist centres where men may follow them and attempt to touch them. Festival nights are particularly bad for this, but it is always best to be accompanied at night, especially when travelling by rickshaw or taxi in towns.

The most important measure to ensure respect is to dress appropriately, in loose-fitting, non-see-through clothes, covering shoulders, arms and legs (such as a *salwaar kameez*, which can be made to fit in around 24 hrs for around Rs 400-800). Take advantage, too, of the gender segregation on public transport, to avoid hassle and to talk to local women.

The best response to staring, whether lascivious or simply curious, is to avert your eyes down and away. This is not the submissive gesture it might seem, but an effective tool to communicate that you have no interest in any further interaction. Aggressively staring back or confronting the starer can be construed as a come-on.

If you are harassed, it can be effective to make a scene. Be firm and clear if you don't wish to speak to someone, and be prepared to raise an alarm if anything unpleasant threatens.

Travel advice

It is better to seek advice from your consulate than from travel agencies. Before you travel you can contact: **British Foreign & Commonwealth Office Travel Advice Unit**, T0845-850 2829, www.fco.gov.uk. **US State Department's Bureau of Consular Affairs**, USA, T202-647 1488, http://travel.state.gov. **Australian Department of Foreign Affairs Canberra**, Australia, T02-6261 3305, www.smartraveller.gov.au. Canadian official advice is on www.voyage.gc.ca.

Theft

Theft is not uncommon. It is best to keep TCs, passports and valuables with you at all times. Don't regard hotel rooms as being automatically safe; even hotel safes don't guarantee secure storage. Avoid leaving valuables near open windows even when you are in the room. Use your own padlock in a budget hotel when you go out. Pickpockets and other thieves operate in the big cities. Crowded areas are particularly high risk. Take special care of your belongings when getting on or off public transport.

If you have items stolen, they should be reported to the police as soon as possible. Keep a separate record of vital documents, including passport details and numbers of TCs. Larger hotels will be able to assist in contacting and dealing with the police. Dealings with the police can be very difficult and in the worst regions, such as Bihar, even dangerous. The paperwork involved in reporting losses can be time consuming and irritating and your own documentation (eg passport and visas) may be demanded.

In some states the police occasionally demand bribes, though you should not assume that if procedures move slowly you are automatically being expected

to offer a bribe. The traffic police are tightening up on traffic offences in some places. They have the right to make on-the-spot fines for speeding and illegal parking. If you face a fine, insist on a receipt. If you have to go to a police station, try to take someone with you.

If you face really serious problems (eg in connection with a driving accident), contact your consular office as quickly as possible. You should ensure you always have your international driving licence and motorbike or car documentation with you.

Confidence tricksters are particularly common where people are on the move, notably around railway stations or places where budget tourists gather. A common plea is some sudden and desperate calamity; sometimes a letter will be produced in English to back up the claim. The demands are likely to increase sharply if sympathy is shown.

Senior travellers

Travellers over 60 can take advantage of several discounts on travel, including 30% on train fares and up to 50% on some air tickets. Ask at the time of booking, since these will not be offered automatically.

Smoking

Several state governments have passed a law banning smoking in all public buildings and transport but exempting open spaces. To avoid fines, check for notices.

Student travellers

Full-time students qualify for an ISIC (International Student Identity Card) which is issued by student travel and specialist agencies (eg Usit, Campus, STA) at home. The card allows certain travel benefits such as reduced prices and concessions into certain sites. For details see www.isic.org or contact **STIC Travels**, www.stictravel.com. Those intending to study in India may get a year's student visa (see page 160).

Telephone

The international code for India is +91.

Mobile phones

Practically all business in India is now conducted via mobile phone. Calls and mobile data are incredibly cheap by global standards – local calls cost as little as half a rupee per minute – and if you're in the country for more than a couple of weeks and need to keep in touch it can definitely be worth the hassle to get a local SIM card.

Arguably the best service is provided by the government carrier **BSNL/MTNL** but connecting to the service is virtually impossible for foreigners. Private companies such as **Airtel**, **Vodafone**, **Reliance** and **Tata Indicom** are easier to sign up with, but the deals they offer can be befuddling and are frequently changed. To get the connection you'll need to complete a form, have a local address or receipt showing the address of your hotel, and present photocopies of your passport and visa plus 2 passport photos to an authorized reseller – most phone dealers will be able to help, and can also sell top-up. **Univercell**, www.univercell.in, and **The Mobile Store**, www.themobilestore.in, are widespread and efficient chains selling phones and SIM cards.

India is divided into a number of 'calling circles' or regions, and if you travel outside the region where your connection is based, you will pay higher 'roaming' charges for making and receiving calls, and any problems that may occur –

with 'unverified' documents, for example – can be much harder to resolve.

Land lines

You can still find privately run phone booths, usually labelled on yellow boards with the letters 'PCO-STD-ISD'. You dial the call yourself, and the time and cost are displayed on a computer screen. Cheap rate (2100-0600) means long queues may form outside booths. Telephone calls from hotels are usually more expensive (check price before calling), though some will allow local calls free of charge.

A double ring repeated regularly means it is ringing; equal tones with equal pauses means engaged (similar to the UK). If calling a mobile, you're as likely to hear devotional Hindu music or Bollywood hits coming back down the line as a standard ringtone.

One disadvantage of India's tremendous rate of growth is that millions of telephone numbers go out of date every year. Current telephone directories themselves are often out of date and some of the numbers given in this book will have been changed even as we go to press. Directory enquiries, T197, can be helpful but works only for the local area code.

Time

India doesn't change its clocks, so from the last Sun in Oct to the last Sun in Mar the time is GMT +5½ hrs, and the rest of the year it's +4½ hrs (USA, EST +10½ and +9½ hrs; Australia, EST -5½ and -4½ hrs).

Tipping

A tip of Rs 10 to a bellboy carrying luggage in a modest hotel (Rs 20 in a higher category) would be appropriate. In upmarket restaurants, a 10% tip is acceptable when service is not already included, while in places serving very cheap meals, round off the bill with small change. Indians don't normally tip taxi drivers but a small extra is welcomed. Porters at airports and railway stations often have a fixed rate displayed but will usually press for more. Ask fellow passengers what a fair rate is.

Tourist information

There are **Government of India** tourist offices in the state capitals, as well as state tourist offices (sometimes **Tourism Development Corporations**) in the major cities and a few important sites. They produce their own tourist literature, either free or sold at a nominal price, and some also have lists of city hotels and paying guest options. The quality of material is improving though maps are often poor. Many offer tours of the city, neighbouring sights and overnight and regional packages. Some run modest hotels and midway motels with restaurants and may also arrange car hire and guides. The staff in the regional and local offices are usually helpful. Check www.incredibleindia.org for details of India tourist offices in your country.

Tour operators

UK

Colours Of India, T020-8347 4020, www.partnershiptravel.co.uk. Tailor-made cultural, adventure, spa and cooking tours.
Cox & Kings, T020-7873 5000, www.coxandkings.co.uk. Offer high-quality group tours, private journeys and tailor-made holidays to many of India's regions, from the lavish to the adventurous, planned by experts.
Dragoman, T01728-861133, www.dragoman.com. Overland, adventure, camping.

Exodus, T0845-287 7408, www.exodus.co.uk. Small group overland and trekking tours.
Greaves Tours, T020-7487 9111, www.greavesindia.com. Luxury, tailor-made tours using only scheduled flights. Traditional travel such as road and rail preferred to flights between major cities.
Kerala Connections, T01892-722440, www.keralaconnections.co.uk. Excellent tailor-made tours specializing in South India, including Lakshadweep, with great homestays.
MAHout, T01295-758 150, www.mahoutuk.com. Specializes in boutique hotels.
Steppes Travel, T01285-787557, www.steppestravel.co.uk. Wildlife safaris, tiger study tours and cultural tours with strong conservation ethic.
Trans Indus, T0844 879 3960, www.transindus.com. Upmarket India travel specialists offering tailor-made and group tours and holidays.

India

Banyan Tours and Travels, T0124-456 3800, www.banyantours.com. Pan-Indian operator specializing in bespoke, upmarket travel, with strength in culture, heritage, adventure and wildlife.
The Blue Yonder, T0413-450 2218, www.theblueyonder.com. India's pioneers in responsible travel run wonderful half-day to multi-day trips in Puducherry, Kerala, Sikkim and Rajasthan. Enthusiastic guides and unusual destinations.
Ibex Expeditions, New Delhi, T011-2646 0244, www.ibexexpeditions.com. Responsible tourism company for tours, safaris and treks. Founding member of the Ecotourism Society of India and award-winner for the most innovative tour operator in India.
Indebo India, New Delhi, T011-4716 5500, www.indebo.com. Customized tours and travel-related services throughout India.

Peter and Friends Classic Adventures, T0832-226 8467, www.classic-bike-india. com. An Indo-German company which arranges high-octane tours around South India, Rajasthan and the Himalaya and Nepal on Enfield motorbikes.

Shanti Travel, T011-4607 7800, www. shantitravel.com. Tailor-made tours throughout India.

North America

Alexander and Roberts, T1-800-221-2216, www.alexanderroberts.com. Packages include Kerala spas, houseboats and wildlife, South India and Karnataka, South India and Tamil Nadu, Goa.

Original World, T1888-367 6147, www.originalworld.com. General and spirituality-focused tours, local experts.

Sita World Travel, T1-800-421-5643, www.sitatours.com. Top-end packages like 7-day Ayurveda programmes and Trails of South India tour.

Visas and immigration

Virtually all foreign nationals, including children, require a visa to enter India. The rules regarding visas change frequently, and arrangements for application and collection also vary from country to country, so it is essential to check details and costs with your relevant embassy or consulate.

Visa on arrival

As of 2015 India has brought 113 countries into its visa-on-arrival scheme, which after several bizarre false starts is – at time of writing – almost as simple as it sounds. An e-Visa costs US$60 and is valid for a stay of up to 30 days; the visa cannot be extended, and only permits travel for tourism purposes. Apply at www. indianvisaonline.gov.in, no later than 4 days before your arrival.

How to get a visa

If you want to stay longer or travel for business or study, you'll still need to go through the traditional visa application process. Most consulates have outsourced their visa services: for up-to-date rules, prices and processing times, go to www. vfsglobal.com if you're in Europe or Australia, www.blsindia-canada.com in Canada, or www.in.ckgs.us in the USA.

Consulates remain closed on Indian national holidays. In general, it is easier (though more costly) to apply in advance by post rather than in person, to avoid long waiting times. It's wise to allow a minimum of 15 business days to get your visa – more for journalist and student visas.

Your passport needs at least 1 blank page, and to be valid for 6 months beyond the period of your visit.

If you're applying for your first India visa, there are 2 critical points to note: first, you'll need to source 2 passport photos in a non-standard 2-inch-square size; and second, the helpful checklist is not just for your benefit but an integral part of the application; you need to print and send it with your other forms.

Language

Want to impress your hosts with a few words of Malayalam? Go ahead and try: the Malayalis boast that their language is one of the hardest in India to learn. In contrast to the clipped tones of Hindi, spoken Malayalam gushes forth in a torrent of words, with barely a discernable gap in between. Then there's the matter of negotiating the common, almost unpronounceable, diphthong 'zh'. Forget about Brezhnev, and put your tongue in the position of the English R, with the tip not quite touching the roof of the mouth, and then try to pronounce the Z of 'zoo'. If you make a sound that's halfway between a Z and the S of 'pleasure', you're ready to march up to the nearest banana seller and demand a bunch of *vaazha pazham*.

Malayam words and phrases

English	Malayalam
Basics	
hello, good morning, goodbye	*namaskaaram*
thank you	*nandi*
no, thank you	*venda, nandi*
excuse me, sorry	*kshamikkanam*
yes	*athe/uvvu*
no	*illa/alla*
never mind/that's all right	*kuzhappamilla*
Questions	
what is your name?	*ningalude peru enthaanu?*
my name is …	*ente peru … ennaanu*
pardon?	*enthaa?*
how are you?	*engane undu?*
I am well, thanks, and you?	*enikku sukahamaanu, nandi, ningalkko?*
not very well	*nalla sukhamilla*
where is the …?	*… evide aanu?*
who is?	*aaraanu?*
what is this?	*ithu enthaanu?*
Shopping	
how much?	*enthaanu vila?*
that makes (20) rupees	*ithinu irupathu roopayaanu*
that is very expensive	*athu valare kooduthalaanu*
make it a bit cheaper	*vila kurackanam*
The hotel	
what is the room charge?	*room charge ethra aanu?*
please show the room	*dhayavaayi room kanickaamo?*

is there an air-conditioned room?	*A C room undo?*
is there hot water?	*choodu vellam kittumo?*
… a bathroom/fan/mosquito net…	*…bathroom/fan/kothuku vala…*
is there a large room?	*valiya room undo?*
please clean it	*dhayavaayi vrithiyaakkamo*
are there clean sheets/blanket?	*vrithiyulla sheet/puthappu undo?*
bill please	*bill tharaamo?*

Travel

where's the railway station?	*railway station evide aanu?*
how much is the ticket to Agra?	*aagrayilekkulla ticket charge eth ra aanu?*
when does the Agra bus leave?	*aagrayilekkulla bus eppol purappedum?*
how much?	*ethra?*
left/right	*idathu/valathu*
go straight on	*nere pokoo*
nearby	*aduththu*
please wait here	*dhayavaayi ivide wait cheyyoo*
please come at 8	*dhayavaayi ettu manikku varoo*
quickly	*vegam*
stop	*nilkkoo*

Time and days

right now	*ippol thanne*	today	*innu*
morning	*raavile*	yesterday	*innale*
afternoon	*uchacku*	Monday	*thinka*
evening	*vaikunneram*	Tuesday	*chovva*
night	*raathri*	Wednesday	*budhan*
tomorrow	*naale*	Thursday	*vyaazham*
month	*maasam*	Friday	*velli*
year	*varsham*	Saturday	*shani*
day	*divasam*	Sunday	*njaayar*
week	*aazhcha*		

Numbers

1	*onnu*	14	*wpathinaalu*
2	*randu*	15	*pathinanchu*
3	*moonnu*	16	*pathinaaru*
4	*naalu*	17	*pathinezhu*
5	*anchu*	18	*pathinettu*
6	*aaru*	19	*paththonpathu*
7	*ezhu*	20	*irupathu*
8	*ettu*	100	*nooru*
9	*onpathu*	200	*irunnooru*
10	*paththu*	1000	*aayiram*
11	*pathinonnu*	2000	*randaayiram*

| 12 | panthrandu | 100,000 | laksham |
| 13 | pathimoonnu | | |

Basic vocabulary

big	valiya	open	thuranna
small	cheriya	police station	police station
chemist	marunnu kada	road	road
clean	vrithi ulla	room	room
closed	adachu	shop	kada
cold	thanuppulla	sick (ill)	asukham
day	divasam	silk	pattu
dirty	vrithi illaththa	that	athu
English	english	this	ithu
excellent	ugran	town	pattanam
food/to eat	aahaaram	water	vallam
hot (spicy)	erivulla	what	enthu
hot (temp)	choodulla	when	eppol
luggage	saadhanam	where	evide
medicine	marunnu	which	ethu
newspaper	dhinappathram	who	aaru
of course, sure	theerchayaayum	why	enthu kondu

Food and drink

please show the menu	menu kaanikkamo?
no chillies please	dhayavaayi mulaku idaruthu
sugar/milk/ice	panchasaara/paal/ice
a bottle of water please	oru kuppi vellam tharumo
sweet/savoury	madhuramulla/ruchiyulla
spoon, fork, knife	spoon, fork, kaththi
chicken	kozhiyirachi/chicken
fish	meen
meat	irachi
prawns	konchu/chemmeen
vegetables	pachakkari
aubergine	vazhuthina
cabbage	cabbage
carrots	carrot
cauliflower	cauliflower
mushroom	koon
onion	savaala
okra, ladies' fingers	vendacka
peas	payar
potato	urulakkizhangu
spinach	cheera
plain boiled rice	champaavari choru

Index → *Entries in **bold** refer to maps*

FOOTPRINT

Features

Kerala ebbs by at snail's pace, most picturesquely in the slow-flowing networks of lagoons and rivers that make up its backwaters, where nature grows in such overwhelming profusion that canals sit choked with pretty water-lily thickets and dragonflies bunch in clouds over lotus leaves. Dawn mists drift through canopies made by antique mango and teak trees, as farmers slip their oars into the silent waters, and women's dresses glare extra bright in the reflections of the still glass waters.

In the ramshackle port city of Fort Kochi, it's as if the clocks stopped a few centuries back: wizened traders sift spice in the shadows of derelict go-downs, the churches glow lime white, at the harbour's edge lines of cantilevered Chinese fishing nets swoop for their next catch of silvery sprats, and medieval streets and antique shops thread the route between the tiny blue-tiled synagogue and grand Dutch wooden palace of Mattancherry.

The southern beaches of Kovalam and Varkala are great places to unwind with Ayurvedic massages, but Malabar, in the north, is the real unsung jewel of the state, an outpost of staunch Hindu religiosity and capital of the Muslim Moplah community. Here, hushed families gather at dawn in leafy temple gardens to watch spectacles of the unique, hypnotic temple dance form Theyyam and, come nightfall, the precision athletes of the swashbuckling martial art Kalarippayattu draw their swords.

Switchback turns bear you from the lush green paddy fields of the plains through spindly rubber plantations and blooming coffee-tree forests up to the thick tea-shrub territory of the high mountain villages of Thekaddy and Munnar, whose nature reserves hide tigers and herds of elephant.

David Stott

Best of
Kerala

❶ The backwaters

The tranquil, hypnotic waterworld of
the backwaters is the best place in India
to cast adrift from life, as you watch the
palm-shaded villages ooze by from the
vantage point of a houseboat. Page 53.

❷ Dusk in Fort Kochi

Quiet lanes thread beneath vast spreading
raintrees in the Dutch-Portuguese enclave
of Fort Kochi. A wonderfully relaxed
introduction to India, with a wealth of
converted mansion hotels, the area is at its
magical best around dusk, as the ancient
Chinese fishing nets etch themselves
against a wash of pink sky and food
hawkers set up their stalls. Page 71.

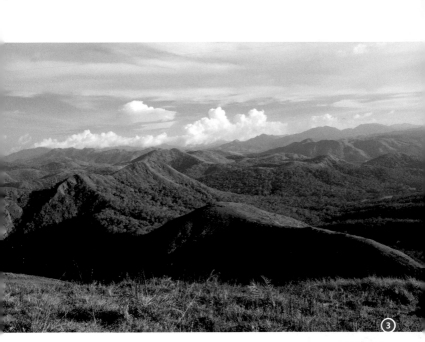

❸ Periyar National Park

Tourists flock to Periyar Lake hoping to catch a glimpse of the park's wild inhabitants from a noisy boat. Avoid them by signing up for one of the excellent guided day walks, led by former poachers, which offer a genuine sense of adventure and the chance to come face to face with wild elephants. Page 89.

❹ Thrissur Pooram

As the summer heat piles on, Kerala's festival season gets into full swing. Thrissur's Pooram is the biggest of them all, a week-long epic of pounding drums, gold-bedecked elephants and non-stop firecrackers. Page 103.

⑤ River Nila

The revered Nila is the birthplace of much of Kerala's high culture, and this little-visited region is a wonderful place to witness classical and folk music. Away from the pore-clogging salt air of the coast, the lush rice-growing country of the Nila is also home to a slew of authentic Ayurvedic resorts. Page 108.

⑥ Wayanad

Blanketed in misty jungles and contoured tea plantations, Wayanad is Kerala's most appealing hill station. Wake up in the arms of a giant tree to the call of Malabar whistling thrush, and spend your days exploring Neolithic rock engravings and towering waterfalls. Page 124.

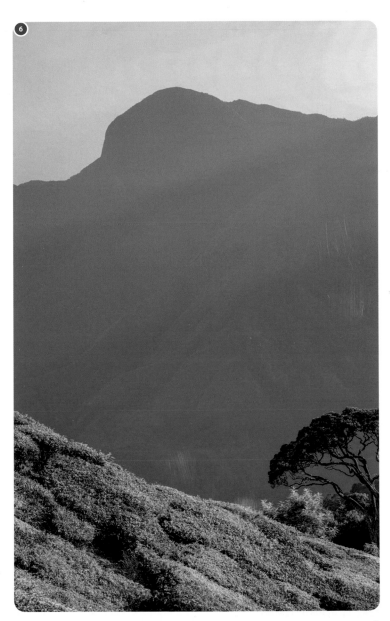

Mudiyettu dancer dressed as the demon Darika